Serving as Senders

Serving as Senders

How to Care for Your Missionaries

Neal Pirolo

Authentic

Copyright © Emmaus Road International, Inc. 1996

Originally published 1991 by Emmaus Road International, Inc.,
7150 Tanner Court, San Diego, CA 92111, U.S.A.

First published 1996 by OM Publishing

12 11 10 09 08 07 06   7 6 5 4 3 2 1

This edition first published 2006 by Authentic Media
9 Holdom Avenue, Bletchley, Milton Keynes, MK1 1QR, UK
And 129 Mobilization Drive, Waynesboro, GA 30830-4575, USA
www.authenticmedia.co.uk
Authentic Media is a division of Send the Light Ltd., a company
limited by guarantee (registered charity no. 270162)

The right of Neal Pirolo
to be identified as the Author of this Work has been asserted by him in
accordance with the Copyright, Designs and Patents Act 1988.

British Library Cataloguing in Publication Data
A catalogue record for this book is available from the British Library

ISBN 1-85078-677-1

Cover design by four-nine-zero design.
Typesetting by Textype, Cambridge
Print Management by Adare Carwin
Printed in Great Britain by J.H. Haynes & Co., Sparkford

Serving As Senders is formatted for individual and group study. The eight study sessions have sections on:

- For Your Personal Involvement
- Actions Steps
- Group Discussion
- For Further Action

The opening stories in Chapters Four and Five are adapted from *In Other Words* January 1977 and October 1990 issues respectively and are used by permission from Wycliffe Bible translators. The opening story in Chapter Eight is adapted from an article by the pastor of Lake Murray Evangelical Free Church and is used by permission. In many stories the names and locations have been changed to protect the innocent (and guilty).

Dedication

To the many
cross-cultural workers
and their support teams
out of whose experiences
come the pages of this book.

Contents

Preface   xi
Acknowledgements   xiii

Chapter 1   The Need for Senders   1

Chapter 2   Moral Support   19

Chapter 3   Logistics Support   44

Chapter 4   Financial Support   64

Chapter 5   Prayer Support   94

Chapter 6   Communication Support   121

Chapter 7   Re-entry Support   137

Chapter 8   Your Part in the Big Picture   164

Epilogue   188

Group Leader's Guide   191

Resources   209

Resources Available Through Emmaus   217
   Road International

Preface

I sat in the upper level of the auditorium at the University of Illinois in Urbana, listening to the heavyweights of the evangelical community challenge 17,000 college students to a vital and personal commitment to world evangelization. It was InterVarsity's Urbana Student Mission Conference.

I must admit I had begun daydreaming when all of a sudden there was that statement: 'In secular war, for every one person on the front line of the battle, there are nine others backing him up in what is called the "line of communication."'

The concept exploded in my mind like a mortar shell! The speaker had been drawing a parallel between secular war and the spiritual warfare that accompanies cross-cultural ministry. He continued, 'And how can we expect to win with any less than that ratio? God is not looking for Lone Rangers or Superstars; He is commanding an army – soldiers of the Cross.'

I said, 'Thank you, Lord, for that confirmation!' At that time I was directing a one-year ministry school that had a strong emphasis on cross-cultural outreach. Though I had had no background in secular war, as soon as students applied to the school, I had been encouraging them to build around themselves a team of *nine* people who would support them in prayer, since enrolling in this school was saying to the enemy, 'I am getting out of the pew and onto the *battlefield*!'

Since that evening at Urbana, with more vigour than ever, I have encouraged, exhorted – even implored – anyone going into cross-cultural outreach ministry not to leave home without a strong, committed support team – a group that accepts the ministry of serving as senders.

By the time we have finished with our study together, you'll be able to answer this question: How can I get involved in the Great Commission of world evangelization even though I know I am called to stay at home?

You can become personally involved in the mission process as a sender.

Ministering by His grace,
Neal Pirolo
San Diego, California

Acknowledgements

Who would have thought that the birthing of such a little book would bring such labour? Yet who would have thought of the joy it also would bring? The coaching team was great! The first acknowledgement must go to the Holy Spirit, our inspiration and Divine Teacher. Second, to my wife Yvonne who often critiqued and rewrote so forcefully that I tried to get her name on the cover. To my brother Paul who didn't laugh when he read through the first draft and used his editing skills to meticulously comb through the final manuscript. To Alice Lovas who co-ordinated and wrote much of the Sacramento church's case study. To the friends of El Adobe Trust who funded the first printing. And even to our kids, for, as our son Byron pointed out, our experiences in raising them have built into us what it took to stay with this project to its completion!

And finally and foremost, *'Now to Him who is able to do immeasurably more than all we can ask or imagine, according to His power that is at work within us'* (Ephesians 3:20).

Chapter One

The Need for Senders

'And how can they preach unless they are sent?'
Romans 10:15

'Beth! Wake up! Please, Beth! Wake up!' Beth's room-mate held the empty Valium bottle in her hand and knew Beth wouldn't wake up. But her instinct told her to get help. The people in the next apartment helped her carry Beth to the car. A mile that seemed half way round the world brought them to the hospital. They pumped Beth's stomach. She stirred and opened her eyes.

Months later Beth could talk about it:

'I had had a normal life before this. Friends, a loving family, a good church life. Basically, I was a happy person. I had been a professional for ten years. I had held reputable positions. I had managed people. And I had managed myself quite well . . . until this.

'I had just returned from a six-month missionary venture in the Far East. My feelings were running rampant. Nostalgia flooded me as I remembered the good times; nightmares and flashbacks haunted me in the quiet solitude

1

of night. Nobody was interested; nobody had time to hear what I had to say.

'I had just come from a fruitful experience as an administrative assistant in a medical clinic. Dumped back into the busy lifestyle of metropolitan Washington, D.C., I lost all sense of identity. Deepening feelings of isolation caused me to withdraw all the more.

'I thought if I got back into my work I could refocus my life. But the emotional instability mounted. One nightmare kept recurring:

'We had been in a village doing some medical work. Through the thundering of a tropical storm, I awoke to the sound of gunfire. Before I could go back to sleep, I saw them dragging the body of a man past the doorway of my hut. The story was that he had been caught in the fields stealing opium.

'Now back in D.C., I would awaken at night to the sounds in my brain of the *pow-pow* of the guns. And the whole ugly scene would flash through my mind again. I began using tranquillizers to control my instability. But before seven or eight in the evening, I was lost in anxiety, confusion, uncertainty – crying uncontrollably.

'Conversely, I also had a sense of "special" knowledge. I was fulfilled by a good missionary experience. Hadn't I *been there*? Hadn't I been successful? Hadn't I bonded with and nurtured Billy to health?

'We had been on our way home from some medical work in the hill country. Along the trail I stumbled on this three-month-old infant. His hands and feet were bound together with rope. He was addicted to opium. He was almost dead. We enquired as best we could whose son he was. His mother already had four children under the age of five.

'The man who was thought to be the father was away on "business" three to four weeks at a time. It was probably this woman who had left him there to die. A couple of hundred yards away was an abandoned hut. We said we would wait there until night-time to talk to his mother. She never came. At the clinic we were able to give him the care he needed. We called him Billy, and he was eventually adopted by a local Christian doctor.

'I became hyper-vigilant about this great need out there. I felt a lot of anger toward people who wouldn't let me talk about my experiences. My pastor wouldn't let me share at church. No Sunday school class had the time for me. My parents couldn't show enough interest even to look at my pictures. I became judgemental and condemning: "How can you be thinking about buying a new car when there are such great needs out there?" But I couldn't say any of that out loud. Hurt, fear, anger and guilt all turned inwards in severe depression. I couldn't sleep at night; I couldn't get out of bed in the morning. I left my job. I took more and more tranquilizers. *I just wanted somebody to acknowledge that I was back home!*

'One Sunday morning after church, I gathered the strength to go again to my pastor and say, "I am at the end of my tether! I think I'm losing it! I need your help!" With his arm around me, he said, "Beth, I am busy. I am so tied up this week. But if you must, call my office to set an appointment for a week from Wednesday. Beth, if you would just get into the Word more. . ."

'Through the dazed fog of an existence I had been living in, all of a sudden it became crystal clear: "Pastor, I'm not worth your time!" I had made other desperate calls to various counsellors. One guy tried to date me. A psychiatrist had given my condition a fancy label. But now it was clear: "I'm not worth anybody's time!"

'I decided to take the rest of the bottle of Valium.'

It would astound most Christians to hear missionaries honestly express their desperate need for support in one area or another. Most pleas aren't as dramatic as Beth's. Yet too many cries for help do end in death. Each appeal speaks of a personal need for those who will come alongside them and serve as senders.

Mission does not just focus on those who go. Those who serve as senders are equally significant.

A Biblical Foundation

If anybody knew about going on missionary journeys and needing a support team, it was the Apostle Paul. He said, '. . . and how can they preach unless they are sent?' In Romans 10 he established the vital importance of cross-cultural outreach on these two levels of involvement: *Those who go* and *those who serve as senders.*

Paul first quoted Joel: 'For whosoever shall call upon the name of the Lord shall be saved.' Then, in the clear, gapless linear logic so well understood by the Roman mind, he appealed: 'How then shall they call on Him in whom they have not believed? And how can they believe in Him of whom they have not heard?'

Today's estimate is that about half of the earth's population has not heard a culturally relevant presentation of the gospel.

'And how shall they hear without a *preacher*?' Yes, there must be a 'preacher' – the missionary, the cross-cultural worker, the *one who goes.* By whatever name and by whatever means he gets there, there must be a proclaimer of the Good News. God chose it to be this way. (Throughout our study, we'll be referring to your missionary with a generic 'he' – though at times we could mean *he, she* or *they!*)

Though the total missions force is decreasing from the Western nations, God is sovereignly raising up an army of workers from the emerging Two-Thirds World countries. But the cry of our Lord two thousand years ago still rings true: 'The harvest is plentiful but the workers are few' (Matthew 9:37). And unfortunately, this is where most mission conferences end their appeal. 'We need more missionaries,' comes their cry.

But wait. There is one more question in this series: 'And how can they preach unless they are *sent?'* (Romans 10:13–15). Paul acknowledged that there are others besides those who go who must be involved in this worldwide evangelization endeavour: those who are serving as senders.

Those who go and those who serve as senders merge their callings and talents and giftings to form the cross-cultural team. All are equally important. All are vitally involved in the fulfilment of the Great Commission. All are dynamically integrated and moving toward the same goal. And all are assured success, for those in God's work are on the winning team!

From the humble beginnings of one hundred young people at the Mount Hermon Meeting of 1886, the Student Volunteer Movement identified and fielded over 20 000 men and women to be *goers* – set apart to declare the gospel and teachings of Christ to a lost world.

This same movement mobilized an army of over 80,000 mission-minded people who pledged themselves to stay at home and support those who went.

In the year 2001 as Guatemala held its first National Missions Conference, the speaker first appealed for those who sensed a call to go to come forward. Then, with equal fervour, he made an appeal for those who would commit their lives to the ministry of serving as senders. Another, even larger group responded.

In decades past, many people grew up in mission-minded churches. Men and women from faraway places came to speak of the challenge to follow in their steps. It was easy for the listener to understand the importance of *those who go*. But they were also left with the feeling that if they were not called to go, the only alternative was to wish them well and say, 'Goodbye!'

This whole scenario, of course, was punctuated with the story of David's men who were too tired to go on, but they would receive an equal share in the spoils. (Read 1 Samuel 30, but don't use it to 'encourage' your support teams!) To those who are already feeling that they are 'second class' because they are not 'giving up everything and going,' this story only punctuates their feelings of not being good enough.

Maybe some people in your fellowship want to be involved in world evangelization but don't feel called to go right now. The good news is there's more they can do than just say goodbye!

There is a tremendous need for *senders*. And the need goes far beyond the traditional token involvement of attending a farewell party or writing out a cheque to missions. A cross-cultural worker needs the support of a team of people while he is preparing to go, while he is on the field and when he returns home.

A careful reading of Paul's missionary letters will reveal how much time he spent talking to his support team – those who were involved with him in the ministry. Sometimes he complimented them, sometimes he expressed his loneliness in being away from them, sometimes he exhorted and challenged them. But he always thanked God for them.

A support team of senders is just as critical to a missionary today. Let's look at some very good reasons why.

A Cross-Cultural Worker's Life Time-Line

Consider this diagram of the physical/emotional/mental/spiritual life time-line of a cross-cultural worker during his missionary experience.

A Cross-Cultural Worker's Life Time-line

A. 'Normal' Living

The flat, horizontal line of this diagram represents the 'normal living' base line of your missionary's existence before he even had a thought about missions. This is not to say that his life was flat! There were the usual ups and downs, but for the purpose of comparison, consider the line as his normal life before missions.

The line resembling the dips and curves of a roller-coaster ride represents the changing emotions of your missionary as he passes through his missionary experience. One veteran said about the ups and downs of missionary life: 'Missionary living takes me on a trip that is totally outside the realm of every comfort zone I have come to enjoy!'

The vertical lines indicate periods of time, milestones along his missionary venture. The relative spaces between the lines may vary due to many factors. But these are expected phases of which you, his support person, should be aware. As you are giving your support, anticipate the next milestone of your cross-cultural worker's life time-line. And be available to offer your assistance.

B. Anticipation of Approval

At some point, your missionary friend emerges from his closet of prayer, having grappled with all the normal feelings of inadequacy. Want to know how he probably felt? Read through Exodus 3 and 4 to hear the patriarch Moses rehearse his five excuses of inadequacy. While you're there, notice that God answers each of those He protests with *His* all-sufficiency.

Boldly or with some reluctance, your friend announced that he believed God had placed a personal call on his life to become a missionary. Every fibre of his being has undergone a rise in excitement and apprehension, visions of grandeur and nightmares of depression.

C. Pre-field Preparation

The day finally comes: the church, missionary society or other responsible body (see Acts 13:1-4) has confirmed that personal call with their approval. It has been deter-mined that your missionary is really going! Through days, weeks, even months of preparation, support-team building, and training, anticipation heightens as the date of departure draws near.

D. Honeymoon Period

Your missionary is catapulted into space in a jet aircraft but his emotions are flying ten metres above the plane. The 'honeymoon' has begun. For a period of time he moves around in a protective bubble, enjoying the novelty of his new life. Even the single control on the shower that produces only cold water is 'interesting.' There is so much to observe, to take in. It's all so . . . different!

E. Culture Stress

The time that passes between these identified stages will vary according to circumstances. But as surely as night follows day, the next stage is inevitable. One morning your missionary rudely awakens to the reality that the single control will never produce hot water! He realizes he has committed himself to circumstances that are no longer quaint; they are now weird, even barbaric!

The adventure of discovery has turned to the dread of 'What next?' The first attack of dysentery keeps him up all night. The fact that this is the most difficult language in the world to learn has him looking for a permanent interpreter. The first hints of persecution or the awareness that people are not going to change as easily or as rapidly as he had hoped have him asking God: 'Why are you doing this to me?' From the pinnacles of ecstasy he has plummeted to the depths of despair. Culture stress has set in.

Most missionaries don't want to talk about this stage of missionary life because people at home won't think of them as 'spiritual' enough if they admit to some of these trying times. It is at this time that your cross-cultural worker needs your support. Many – too many – crash here. Of course, some turn back before they leave the airport!

F. Ministry of Love

But your missionary has been taught that culture stress is a normal stage to go through. As Paul encouraged Timothy, you are there to support your missionary friend through this time of disappointment. Therefore, he will do just that: go through it into a time of ministry motivated by the love of Christ. Because of your strong support he will emerge with a strengthened vision of God's purposes in his life and his reasons for being a missionary. All is not rosy. The adversaries are there. But the 'great door for effective work' that Paul talked about is there, too (see 1 Corinthians 16:9).

G. Anticipation of Return

Life goes on. As surely as this missionary journey had a starting point, the time will come when your cross-cultural worker will, like Paul and Barnabus, return 'to Antioch, where they had been committed to the grace of God for the work they had now completed' (Acts 14:26).

Again, his feelings are mixed. Yes, your missionary wants to come home to see you. But he has made new friends. He has new ideas and ideals. He has different behaviour patterns that he knows will be difficult to integrate into his new home environment. No, he isn't returning to his old home environment when he comes back. For you also have changed!

His heart has been broken with compassion for the lost; and there are so few to take his place in ministry. The desire to stay and continue in ministry usually outweighs the desire to return home. Thus, the emotional/ psychological/spiritual pulse of your missionary drops again.

Probably the shortest letter ever written was to a missionary whose furlough had been booked; all plans had been set. Then, remembering the difficulties of previous times at home he wrote that he had changed his mind; he was not coming. The reply came back: 'Pete! Come home!' He came and his support team was able to help him through the next stage.

H. Cultural Stress in Reverse

In Chapter Seven, we deal extensively with the support your cross-cultural worker needs after his return. The trauma during re-entry is intense. An example is the re-entry desperation of Beth who told her story at the beginning of this chapter. In this great time of need, your missionary might feel especially inadequate to do anything about it.

During this time of reverse culture stress, coming home requires strong support.

I. Full Integration

A missionary who has been trained to anticipate the stress of coming home and has a strong re-entry support team will, in time, fully integrate his changed self into the changed home environment. He will be a positive agent for change in his church and community. He will stay 'a long time with the disciples' (Acts 14:28). He will, like Paul, remain 'in Antioch', teaching and preaching

(Acts 15:35). And who knows? After a while he might even say, 'Hey, Barnabas, let's go out again!' (See Acts 15:36.)

Today no cross-cultural worker should leave home without a strong, integrated, educated, knowledgeable, excited-as-he-is, active team of people who have committed themselves to the work of serving as senders.

You may be a part of that team. Your heart is stirred by people of other cultures, yet you have not heard God's call to go. When a missionary speaks at your church or a breakthrough is reported, there is a quickening of your pulse. Yet you know God has directed you to stay at home. You may be called to the ministry of serving as a sender.

Prayerfully consider serving as a sender in one or more of six areas of support:

Moral Support – a word of encouragement
Logistics Support – all the bits and pieces
Financial Support – money, money, money
Prayer Support – spiritual warfare at its best
Communication Support – letters, tapes and more
Re-entry Support – more than applauding
    the safe landing of his jumbo jet

Each area has its unique responsibilities; each is best served by specific gifts within the body of Christ. Allow His Spirit to speak to your heart about your possible involvement in one of these phases of support.

The gift of administration will be very helpful for logistics support. To contribute to the financial support of your friend will be easier if you have the gift of giving. Vital to prayer support is the gift of intercession. Re-entry support is greatly helped by those who exercise the gift of hospitality. Allow His Spirit to speak to your heart about your possible involvement in one of these areas of support.

God's call on your life to serve as a sender must be just as vibrant as the call on the life of the one you send. Likewise, the commitment you make must be as sure as that of your cross-cultural worker. The responsible action you take is as important as the ministry your field worker undertakes.

And the reward of souls for His Kingdom will be equal to your missionary's and your own faithfulness.

A Case Study in Support

As a church in Sacramento, California, began preparations to send their second missionary family, the concept of the church serving as senders became a priority. Seven couples committed themselves to direct the support team for Lou and Sandy and their six-month-old baby girl Marlies.

Each one on the team was encouraged to consider the responsibilities of each area of support. One of the team members tells the story:

Lou and Sandy invited nine couples to their home in June. They had already been to the Philippines. They had visited several ministries there – trusting that the Lord would show them where he wanted them to serve.

At the June meeting, Lou shared with us the opportunity they sensed God had provided for them. 'But' he said, 'the only way we will be able to go is if we have a core group responsible for our support.' He discussed the basic needs for moral, logistics, financial, prayer, communication and re-entry support and how the core group would head up each of these areas. He then asked us to pray seriously about being a part of this team effort. He wanted our answer within two weeks. As it turned out, seven couples felt God's calling to serve. That was our beginning.

We all knew we wanted to support Lou and Sandy. After all, we had said we would be a part of the core group. But what was next? As Lou had asked George and me to head up the core group, we phoned the others to see if there was any specific area of ministry they would like to be involved in. The Hughes would head the logistics support. The Huffmans had a heart for re-entry. The Martins wanted to be responsible for communication support. Others responded in turn.

We had our first real meeting as a core group in August. At first I think we wanted to appear as if we had it 'all together'. As the meeting progressed, however, it became apparent that in fact we hadn't. But praise God, the barriers began to break down and we were able to admit that we were confused in some areas. As we began to discuss our problems, we also began to brainstorm as a group and to explore possible answers.

So here's an opportunity for you to serve as a sender, to be a vital part of the mission process.

Hang on! As we'll see in the next chapter, there's more to it than raising your hand to volunteer. As your cross-cultural worker encounters difficulties, your moral support is needed to protect him.

(In addition to the following individual study, see the **Group Leader's Guide** for Session One beginning on page 191.)

For Your Personal Involvement

Throughout this study you will find many Scripture references. To benefit more fully from the lessons, read each one in its full context. Allow the Holy Spirit to 'guide you into all truth' (John 16:13).

● Read Romans 10:13–15. From that passage fill in the blanks in the following statement. Notice that there is a key word in each question that leads you to the next question. The foundation of the whole sequence, then, lies in the final word!

10:13 Everyone who ———— on the name of the Lord will be saved (see Joel 2:32).

10:14 How, then, can they ———— on the one they have not ———— ? And how can they ———— in the one of whom they have not ———— ? And how can they without ————— ?

10:15 And how can they ———— unless they are ——— ? (Write that final word in capital letters to highlight in your mind the importance of serving as senders!)

● List the nine stages of the physical/emotional/ psychological/spiritual life time-line of a missionary, and the incident in time that forms the transition from one to another. (Note the example.)

Period A:	Normal Living:	personal call
Period B:	—————;	—————
Period C:	—————;	—————
Period D:	—————;	—————
Period E:	—————;	—————
Period F:	—————;	—————
Period G:	—————;	—————
Period H:	—————;	active in ministry
Period I:	—————;	

- Read the following passages relating to Paul's need for a support team. Write in each space the type of support Paul was either asking for or expressing thanks for – whether moral, logistics, financial, prayer, communication or re-entry. Following the semi-colon, place the gifting that would make serving in this area easier. (Each area is referred to in at least one passage.)

  Ephesians 6:18–19 _____ ;
  2 Timothy 4:13 _____ ;
  Acts 14:26–28 _____ ;
  Acts 21:12–13 _____ ;
  Romans 16 _____ ;
  Philippians 4:10–12 _____ ;

- Indicate on the following pedestals where you think 'cultural Christianity' estimates the value of:
  - Pastor
  - Lay person
  - Missionary
  - Evangelist

Did you put the lay person on the lowest stand?

● Now read 1 Corinthians 1:11–13; 3:4–9; 12:12–27 and Revelation 2:6,15

After prayer, fill in the following sentence:

I, _____ as a sender,
              (your name)

am as important in God's global plan (but not more important) as _____, even though
              (name a famous missionary)
my role won't seem as dramatic.

Maybe you don't feel able to fill that in just now. Go ahead and read through *Serving As Senders*. By the end of our study, we trust you will be able to make that statement personal!

Action Steps

By the time you have read Chapter One, completed the 'For Your Personal Involvement' section and participated in a group discussion (See **Group Leader's Guide** beginning on page 191), you should:

● Be aware of the need for those who serve as senders.
● Want to explore further to know where you might fit in.
● Take the initiative. Let your missionary friend know that you are learning about the ministry of serving as a sender. And you will soon be available to help support him in one or more areas for God's glory!

- Involve others. Look among your fellowship for those who seem to be at loose ends. Possibly they are the cross-cultural parts of your church. Invite them to read and study this book with you.

Chapter Two

Moral Support

*'Be strong and courageous. Do not be terrified;
do not be discouraged, for the LORD your
God will be with you wherever you go.'*
Joshua 1:9

'It was a bit unusual. The rapid sequence of events, that is. We trained others to assume our ministries in the church, got married, attended a 12-week field training course in Tijuana, Mexico, and spent our first year together living on a kibbutz in Israel!

'But why not? We were young, adventurous and had not yet accumulated a lot of possessions. And most of all, the church where we had been ministering for the past three years was totally supportive. It was a small fellowship in a small town, so everyone knew us. The smiles and hugs on Sunday morning said to us, "Scott and Jean, this is right!" Deep in our own hearts, God's peace said, "This is right!"

'Invitations to our wedding included a note saying, "No gifts, please; we are going to Israel!" "This is right!" they said with their donations of money instead. A prayer of blessing by our pastor at the wedding said, "This is right!" Even our non-Christian parents said, "This is right!" The moral support from every quarter said, "This is right!"

'We began our training in Tijuana. We met our Mexican host family. Classes began. Learning how to relate to each other – we had been married just four weeks – was the subject of one of the classes. We did our field work in the community, grappling with cultural adaptation and relating to our host family with our limited Spanish. But with their patience and a lot of humour, we learned how to learn a second language and we bonded with them. Principles of spiritual warfare were preparing us for battle. We were learning how to live and minister in a second culture. Communication from our home church assured us that the sense of God's direction was solid. "This is right," we said to each other.

'Then, as a part of our training to make sure the support system was "up and running", we were sent home for a long weekend. We sat in the pastor's living room. Somehow there was an awkwardness. We glanced at each other: "This is not right!" we thought.

'Then Pastor Joe spoke: "Scott and Jean, I have made the decision that you are not to continue in this mission!"

'We were stunned. Our objections were not too well thought-out and they probably didn't make much sense since we were so confused. My wife started crying. Pastor Joe said firmly, "Jean, I am not moved by your tears!" We were speechless! We became angry but he remained firm: "You are not to go! If you continue, you are on your own!"

'We were dazed. The bottom had just fallen out of our world. The whole basis of our support team was shattered! There was a very empty feeling in the pit of our stomachs. We could hardly go to church. We weren't allowed to contact any of the people there for further support. "This is not right!" we knew.

'Fortunately, a part of our support team was made up of individuals from several other churches and Bible study groups. As we all beseeched the Lord for His direction in this new situation, we came to believe that it wasn't that we shouldn't go, but that we were losing a vital part of our support team.

'Just before leaving for Israel, by chance we met Pastor Joe downtown. He was so convinced that God had spoken to him that he said if we continued on this venture, something bad was going to happen to us in Israel. He would stake his ministry on it!

'Needless to say, this added insult to injury. Not only had we lost a strong foundation of moral support, but now this prediction was to cause a continual cloud of apprehension during our whole trip. When anything risky or unknown loomed ahead, we would remember his statement. For example, one night at the kibbutz, we were awakened by a loud siren. We were ready to run for the bomb shelter as we had often practised. "This is it! What bad thing is going to happen to us?" we thought. But since we saw no one else running and the siren stopped, we went back to bed.

'The next day we discovered that the temperature in the turkey house had fallen below a safe level. The siren was to alert the men responsible to adjust the thermostat! Though the humour of that situation mellowed our apprehension, Pastor Joe's cloud of doom hovered above every crisis.

'We have now returned home. It was a successful time of ministry in Israel. We're finding that God is slowly healing our relationships with the people of that church. Pastor Joe did not leave his ministry – in fact, he recently allowed us to share in a local outreach from his church!'

Moral support is the very foundation of the support system. Everyone in the church can be involved in this part of the ministry since in its most basic concept, moral support is simply saying, 'God bless you! We are excited with you in your missionary venture!'

Did the great men and women of the Bible need moral support? Let's look at a few of them.

But David Found Strength in the Lord

Jesse's seven other sons had been rejected. For 'The Lord does not look at the things man looks at. Man looks at the outward appearance, but the Lord looks at the heart.' There remained one – a boy. A teenager. They brought him in from the fields where he was tending the sheep. And the Lord said, 'Rise and anoint him; he is the one.' And the Spirit of the Lord was on David from that day forward.

Through the battle with Goliath, through the struggle with Saul's insane jealousy, through the war of nerves during the months and years of fleeing and being pursued by a king who was troubled by an evil spirit, through the conflict involved in building his royal entourage of six hundred ruthless men, the Spirit of the Lord was upon David (see 1 Samuel 17–29).

And as the Philistines were assembled against Israel, David and his men were with them. But a distrust of these Hebrews troubled the minds of the Philistines (see 1 Samuel 29). David and his men were sent back to Ziklag – only to discover that the Amalekites had invaded from the south, burned the city and carried away all their wives and children. And they wept 'until they had no strength left to weep . . . David was greatly distressed because the men were talking of stoning him. But David found strength in the Lord' (see 1 Samuel 30).

Imagine the intensity of the moment – the physical distress of a three-day return march to Ziklag. The adrenalin flow building up to a battle against Israel and then the let-down. The bombarding emotions of losing family and possessions. The internal battle of 'Lord, I am your anointed king of Israel. When am I going to possess the throne?' Where was David's moral support team? They wanted to stone him!

But David found strength in the Lord.

My Hour Has Come

Eleven hundred years later. Another man, another occasion. He says to His three-man support team, 'My soul is overwhelmed with sorrow to the point of death. Stay here and keep watch with Me' (Matthew 26:38). And now the Godman, the propitiation for our sins, 'the Lamb slain from the creation of the world' enters the most significant arena of battle of all time.

The battle of wills rages. All His humanness rises to say, 'Father, there must be another way. I cannot drink this cup of separation. We have been eternally One. Isn't there another way to redeem man back to You? Let this cup pass from Me!'

The anguish becomes intense, for He knows there is no other way. The mental and spiritual suffering of the incarnate God in atonement for the sins of fallen man leads Him to the extreme of physical torture: the bloody sweat.

'Could you men not keep watch with Me for one hour?' Jesus questioned His followers. Twice and then a third time He came to them: 'The hour has come!'

In each of these situations there were those who could have been supportive. But David's men, so overcome by their own loss of wives and children and homes, thought only to stone David. Christ's men, self-indulgent in sleep, were not even aware of their Master's passion that night.

What of the others? When Joseph found that Mary was pregnant by the Holy Spirit, his first response was to 'put her away privately.' In John 9, Jesus compassionately healed a blind man. When the Jewish elders wanted the parents' testimony in support of their son's healing, in fear they said, 'Ask him! He's old enough to tell you!' When Paul was determined to go to Jerusalem, people at two different times tried to dissuade him – even insisting on one occasion that the Holy Spirit had instructed them to warn him.

The pages of history do not paint a brighter picture. Through the centuries, the pattern has not changed. Read about the bold men and women God told to go to the nations in Ruth Tucker's biographical history of Christian missions, *From Jerusalem to Irian Jaya* (see Resources, page 208). You can count on the fingers of one hand the few who found strong moral support for their pioneer vision.

An English cobbler named William Carey struggled in the 1790s with the Church's responsibility to the Great Commission. Later he was to become known as the 'Father of Modern Missions.' But in his early days as the vision stirred deep in his heart, there was no support. His fellow churchmen openly rebuked him by saying, 'When God pleases to convert the heathen, He will do it without your aid or ours.' His wife initially refused to join him on his voyage to India. Only a delay in the departure date gave her the opportunity to reconsider.

Today as thousands of cross-cultural workers grapple with the issues of being His soldiers of the cross in another culture, what sort of moral support can they anticipate from people?

- People so lost in their own narrow world that they do not support God's anointed but rather begin hurling stones of incrimination – like David's men?
- People lulled into self-indulgent sleep to such an extent that they are unaware of God's plan for their friends – like Christ's men?
- People so concerned about public opinion that they want to nod nicely at missionary zeal but try to send their worker away privately – like Joseph?
- People so afraid for the other programmes of their church that they don't want anything to do with daring adventures into the unknown, the uncomfortable? Mission ministry, after all, could be regarded as competition to the status quo – according to moral-non-supporters like the Jewish elders.
- People so sure that they have 'heard from the Lord' that the missionary's 'hearing from the Lord' is wrong – like Paul's friends?
- People who pierce God's missionary heart by distorting their theology – like Carey's friends?

Attitudes and Actions That Do Not Support

Stones of incrimination. Some cannot handle the personal challenge presented by a friend who thinks God wants him to do such a bold, daring thing as go to the mission field. Whether ignorantly, out of well-meaning friendship or to assuage their own feelings of distress, they may begin hurling stones of incrimination: 'But it's a rough world out there! Riots and wars! Hatred and violence! You could get yourself killed!'

Other insensitive responses might include 'You must be joking! You? A missionary? What do you think you can do to save the world?'

Often close, loving friends counsel:

- You're needed here. You have so much to offer right here in our fellowship.
- Waste your education out in the middle of nowhere? What will your parents say?
- Why don't you get a real job? Make some money so you'll be secure; later on you can think about getting involved in missions.
- You can't upset your mother like this. How can you take her grandchildren away from her? They need her!
- What about your kids' education? They will come home ignoramuses and social misfits!
- You expect to get married out there? You'll never meet anybody!

In a final lament, abandoning all logic, they may cry, 'I don't believe this is happening to me!'

The cross-cultural worker who has already battled it out with the Lord over feelings of inadequacy sits in a dishevelled heap – beneath a pile of stones, battered and hurting. The few and the strong who make it find strength in the Lord. But it would be so much better if they had you as a part of their Moral Support Team to encourage them.

Self-indulgent sleep is the state of too large a section of today's Church. Self-indulgence has produced a myopic introspection; we seem to focus on healing ourselves so we can have nicer lives. 'Lord, comfort me so that I will be comfortable' is in direct contrast to what the Church is told in 2 Corinthians 1:4 (and throughout Scripture).

We want to be comfortable and we want security. We feel uneasy about unpredictability – like Peter as he blurted in his threatened loss of security, 'Never, Lord! . . . This shall never happen to you!' (Matthew 16:22).

Perhaps the 'Barnabas and Saul' of your fellowship come back from a Student Missionary conference, a two-week mini-mission or a summer of service sensing the greatness of God's plan of the ages and their privileged part in it. Perhaps in your church, as in too many others, few barely rouse themselves to hear these enthusiasts report on what God is doing globally. As the Church nods off, the potential missionaries say, 'Could you not listen for just one minute to what I believe God has in store for us?'

The cross-cultural worker goes back to the Rock and prays again, 'Father, there must be some other way for you to accomplish your purpose than by having me go.'

'No, my child. This is the way. Walk in it.' And his hour comes. No support is given. All scatter. And the cross-cultural worker faces the Judases and priests and mobs of this world on his own – unless you are there to give him your moral support.

Worries about public opinion can hurt a missionary. Perhaps the potential cross-cultural worker is told, 'OK, if you must go, go. But don't rock the boat. Don't get people here involved – especially financially. What will happen to our other projects?'

Fortunately, it is getting harder and harder for churches to have this attitude because missionary societies and those agencies helping to prepare cross-cultural workers for service are insisting that the local fellowship take the initiative in the missions process.

However, tragically, there are still thousands of cases in which a mission candidate's pastor is the 'last to know.' Or perhaps he never finds out! Public opinion in some churches does not allow for radical moves into international evangelization. So the cross-cultural worker has to leave very quietly – unless you are there to shout an encouraging, 'Bon voyage!'

Other attitudes dry up your cross-cultural worker's supply of moral support.

Competition within the body of Christ scares some fellowships into undermining a mission candidate's moral support. The message might be very strong: 'We don't want to lose you.'

It wasn't that the Jews did not believe in world evangelization. For Christ said of them, 'You travel over land and sea to win a single convert' (Matthew 23:15). Nor was it that they were against His healing people. But throngs of people were following Jesus. He was a threat to the establishment. He was the competition. He didn't fit into their programmes.

The bold, the daring, the assertive plans of the world missionary community don't fit into the programmes of a lot of today's churches, either – unless you are there to encourage Christ's example of unity in diversity.

Contradictory counsel can discourage a missionary. The Apostle Paul sensed at every turn the potential of the enemy's move. 'I will stay on at Ephesus until Pentecost, because a great door for effective work has opened to me and there are many who oppose me' (1 Corinthians 16:8,9). At Miletus he wrote, 'compelled by the Spirit, I am going to Jerusalem, not knowing what will happen to me there. I only know that in every city the Holy Spirit warns me that prison and hardships are facing me' (Acts 20:22,23). The one who is boldly doing the work of the Lord is left alone – unless you are there to provide moral support to sustain your missionary in his difficult times when the adversaries are opposing him.

Distorted theological views can end up damaging the morale of a cross-cultural worker. The missionary heart of God is pierced again and again as fellowships deny the biblical injunctions to go and preach and teach.

Some shout it as brashly as did William Carey's contemporaries: 'God will do it without us if He wants it done!' Others say it more subtly: 'We're too young as a fellowship. We're not big enough yet. No one in our fellowship seems interested. We don't have the resources to support a missionary. I don't have the time to devote to another new project. We would only want to send our best, and we can't afford to lose our leadership.'

Those excuses and a thousand more have all been thought or spoken. Yet not one of them stands the test of exposure to Scripture. Each excuse shrinks into the shadows, trying to hide from the light of His Word. There is no theology to deny the missionary heartbeat of our God who is 'not wanting anyone to perish, but everyone to come to repentance' (2 Peter 3:9).

Therefore, the cross-cultural parts of the body – and there are cross-cultural parts, or else it is not a body – hang lifeless in atrophy for lack of exercise. Or if they are challenged by another church or society, their home church is jealous because they are drawn away. And we are all the losers for it.

The story is told of a young sailor who was making final preparations for a solo voyage around the world in his homemade craft. Throngs of people crowded the small mooring as he stowed away the last boxes of provisions. A murmuring air of pessimistic concern exploded into a volume of discouragement: 'Son, you'll never make it! That boat will not withstand the waves of the storms! You'll run out of food! The sun will fry you!'

A late arriver, hearing all these discouraging warnings, felt an irresistible desire to offer some optimism and encouragement. As the little craft began sailing away from the pier, he pushed his way to the end of the dock.

Waving his hands wildly, he kept shouting, 'Bon voyage! You're really somebody! We're with you! We're proud of you! God be with you, brother!'

The world seems to offer two kinds of support: 'Wait till you get out in that cold, cruel world. It's rough!' And those who exude a contagious, confident 'Bon voyage!'

There are dozens of thoughtless ways to burst the balloon of your aspiring missionary. But there are also plenty of ways you can buoy up his enthusiasm with solid moral support.

Some Holy Spirit-guided soul-searching of your own attitudes toward cross-cultural ministry would be good at this point. An initial clearing of these negative thoughts and actions will allow you to lay a foundation for building a strong support system for the cross-cultural outreach ministry of your church.

How to Give Solid-As-A-Rock Moral Support

Dan had heard the call of God to go. He had visited Thailand on several occasions. There he had seen the hunger of pastors to learn to study the Word. He had experienced the joy of helping them satisfy that hunger through the seminars he taught.

And now Dan was sure God was directing him to a longer-term commitment: to establish a ministry conducting seminars for national pastors of Asia, seminars designed to train pastors in the study of the Word of God, thus allowing them better to feed their flocks.

But Dan was the pastor of a church in the United States. It would not be easy to leave. He had founded the church. Who would fill his position? How could he uproot his family and move them into the unknown?

What about the finances and logistics of that move? What about communication and prayer? Where would they live when they came home?

All of these questions and apprehensions were real and needed answers. But they were more easily handled because the entire congregation gave their full moral support to what they sensed from the Lord to be a 'new thing' for Dan and for them!

Moral support is the foundation of the sending process. Moral support is the 'Bon voyage' of those who serve as senders to those who go. Moral support is as much an attitude that your cross-cultural worker will sense as an action you can perform.

Let's look at some solid foundation stones.

Jesus is the Chief Cornerstone

First, of course there has to be a cornerstone, '. . . a tested stone, a precious cornerstone, for a sure foundation' (Isaiah 28:16). In Jesus' day, the cornerstone was not some memorial plaque set into the wall after the building was completed. It was the first stone laid. All measurements of height, length and breadth were taken from it. If it were well-placed, the building had a good chance of being well-constructed. But if it were poorly laid, watch out!

Christ's life and teachings were an example of moral support. In fact, when Matthew wrote his gospel, the Holy Spirit inspired him to recall how Jesus fulfilled Isaiah's prophecy. 'A bruised reed he will not break, and a smouldering wick he will not snuff out' (Matthew 12:20 quoting Isaiah 42:3). A more modern rendering is, 'He does not crush the weak, nor snuff out the smallest candle flame'. 'He doesn't kick you when you're down!' might be an appropriate paraphrase.

What Does He Do?

He takes the bruised reed by the hand and, lifting her up, says, 'Where are they? Has no one condemned you? Then neither do I condemn you. Go now and leave your life of sin' (John 8:10,11). He meets the 'smoking flax' at night since Nicodemus feared the Jews; he gently breathes the Spirit of life into the newly burning soul (John 3:1–21). Simon Peter's tears of remorse had all but extinguished his flame of fire. Jesus tenderly fans those failing embers back to life with His trilogy of poignant questions: 'Simon, do you love me? Feed my sheep!' (John 21:15–18).

His example of refusing to condemn and determining to encourage is the cornerstone of our support structure as we serve as senders. But it's not enough just to do His deeds. No amount of human-level determination will equip you to be an adequate sender if you're not an intimate disciple of Jesus Christ. This topic is beyond our focus of study, but every sender, every sending team must be personally, constantly communing with the One who in moral support told us, 'As the Father has sent me, I am sending you' (John 20:21). *The Jesus Style*, a book by Gayle D. Erwin gives valuable and practical instruction on this subject (see Resources, page 212).

The Simplicity of Moral Support

The cornerstone has been laid. We can begin building. The first foundation stone that nudges right up and fits so perfectly beside the chief cornerstone is the moral support of the church that helps cross-cultural workers to 'Do it simply – and simply do it!'

Jesus was a master at reducing to simplicity the impassioned issues of His day – and ours.

On the complex issue of taxation, He said, 'Whose image is on the coin?'

'Caesar's,' was the answer.

'Well, you had better give it to him then. But also give to God what belongs to Him!'

We spend hours questioning what life is all about. Where did we come from? Jesus simply said, 'I came from the Father.' We spend days wondering why we're here. Jesus said, 'I am doing the will of the Father.' We spend years worrying where we're going. Jesus said, 'I am going to the Father.' In simple yet precise terms, He answered the three universal questions of life! (See John 13:1–15.)

Jesus' ministry was deep, yet simple. And His lifestyle was also simple. He was born in a stable. He had no place to call home. His body occupied a borrowed tomb at His death.

As your cross-cultural worker begins taking the steps toward the fields of the world, a thousand opportunities and ways to minister will begin bombarding him. Encourage him to keep his eyes focused on the simple, straightforward ministry of Jesus. Urge him to listen quietly to the direction of the Spirit out of all the godly counsel he is receiving (see Proverbs 19:20–21). Remind him to keep it simple; he's not some new messiah! Advise him also simply to do it – to keep going one step at a time.

Help him practise a 'wartime lifestyle' even before going abroad. This doesn't mean living under an austere, ascetic vow of poverty. It means trimming off what isn't necessary. It means not spending on some things and spending strategically on others – much as a soldier going into combat doesn't need a gold-embossed jogging suit but does need a very expensive, state-of-the-art rifle.

Encouraging simplicity in ministry goals and in lifestyle is moral support!

Integrating Missions

The next foundation stone also fits snugly in its place. Support your worker in his perspective that mission is an integrated ministry of the church. Cross-cultural outreach is not the only God-ordained ministry.

'Yes, it is exciting to see that God has chosen you to minister cross-culturally. Yes, the zeal of the Lord is upon you,' you can agree with your missionary friend. But then you must remind him that the Sunday school teachers who tolerated his primary school age distractions are now dealing with the next generation of potential missionaries. Therefore, their work continues to be vital.

All the parts of the body work together in one direction within the 'unchangeable purpose of God' (see Hebrews 6:11–18), each adding its own expertise. Some of these ministries relate directly to that ultimate purpose of the Church – to bless with the Good News every people, tribe and tongue. And some are indirectly related.

You can encourage your missionary to remember that an accurate, big-picture world-view integrates ministries; it doesn't eliminate some nor value one ministry above another.

God's great purpose incorporates every God-given discipline in your life, every ministry in the life of your church. For example:

When your church members visit the elderly they can mention specific prayer requests of the urgent needs of all the ministries of the church. They can teach the elderly how to pray against the strongholds of Satan over a particular people group your missionary is targeting. They can infuse into each housebound person's remaining days a sense of purpose – 'You can spend time in prayer that we can't! You know more about life than we do; therefore you can pray specifically for the ups and downs of our mission team. You can help open the way for the gospel in this group as you pray against the principalities and powers that rule and blind them! We need you!' A church ministry to housebound individuals can be incorporated into the vision of Christ's global cause, whether they pray for your missionary or for the church's prison ministry.

Every God-ordained ministry of the Church can be expanded as it aligns its purposes with the great, unchangeable purpose of God. The life of the whole body – not just the cross-cultural parts – must remain strong. Therefore, the worship leaders must continue to usher us into the very throne room of God, and the Bible teachers must continue to feed the flock. And the other outreach ministries of the Church must continue to reach out.

This is not easy for a missionary to appreciate as he gets into his ministry. His part of the big picture of God's purpose can easily become the only activity he sees. Therefore, you enter as his moral supporter to give him a godly perspective.

You are able to help him recognize that moral support is a two-way street: to enjoy the moral support of others demands that he is interested in and an encouragement to them in their endeavours.

Active Listening

Another foundation stone of moral support is the art of active listening. Paul Tournier in his book *To Understand Each Other* said, 'Most conversations of this world are "dialogues of the deaf."' Emotional isolation is already a major problem in the UK. So when your friend is grappling with all the uncertainties of moving into cross-cultural outreach ministry, he needs even greater support: he needs your listening ear.

When your friend shares his thoughts about cross-cultural involvement, your ministry of moral support is most effective as you simply sit and listen.

Active listening is probably one of the most neglected foundation stones of moral support. Active listening says, 'I am with you. I will take the time. I will put energy into really listening to your heart, not just to what your surface words are saying.'

Active listening calls for all your attention. It is hard work; it requires concentration. But how necessary it is to moral support!

Active listening demands that you respond with respect. Even though you are not 'in his shoes' and cannot fully comprehend what he is experiencing, you can express empathy. Try to sense his thoughts and feelings as he anticipates his venture of faith.

Active listening demands feedback. Repeat in your own words what you heard him say. For example, imagine yourself listening to Scott and Jean after their traumatic meeting with Pastor Joe as recounted at the beginning of this chapter.

Scott says, 'Then Pastor Joe spoke and said, "I have made the decision that you are not to continue in this mission!" We were stunned!'

You respond, 'I guess you were!'

'No kidding,' says Jean, 'I guess our objections were not too well thought-out.'

You say, 'You mean your objections to his objections?'

Jean laughs. 'Yeah, I guess so. What we said probably didn't make much sense since we were so confused.'

You respond, 'Your thoughts were too scattered to explain to him how you knew God wants you to go.'

'Right,' says Scott. 'We know how to explain it to people now after that experience!'

'Does it feel good to be confident about God's direction?' you ask.

Jean says, 'It really does – despite Pastor Joe's response . . .'

And you've effectively listened through a painful experience that needed to be shared. You've also allowed Scott and Jean to work through some of their feelings about the incident until they begin to have some positive feelings about it. Your active listening and repeating what you thought you heard has resulted in a great show of solid moral support!

Just a word of encouragement and to listen with positive feedback helps your missionary clarify his thoughts and feelings on a host of new concepts he must process.

We all know the risks of international travel. We all know the dangers of terrorist activity. We all know the socio-political issues related to the rise in nationalism. We all know the fears of the unknown. God does, too. Yet He says, 'Go!'

Will you be one of those who will say, 'Wow! What a privilege to be about our Father's business!'? Will you offer, 'We're with you! What can we do to help?' You can be one who shouts, 'God bless you! We're proud of you! You're really something! Bon voyage!'

Stone by stone, the foundation of moral support is being laid.

Commissioning as Moral Support

There may be other stones of solid moral support that His Spirit will bring to your mind. But for now let's consider three more stones that are vital to this foundation: confirmed, strategy determined and commissioned. The church in Antioch provides a model from which we can draw our examples.

They put five men forward; they fasted and prayed. They heard the Holy Spirit say, 'We want Barnabas and Saul.' They fasted and prayed some more; they laid their hands on them. They sent them away. Who is 'they'? The church, the local body of believers – those who were sharing their own concern for this ministry that was burning deep in the hearts of Barnabas and Saul (see Acts 13).

Confirmed

The church, the home group, the missions fellowship, the prayer group, the college and career class – some group besides the ones wanting to go need to hear the Holy Spirit say, 'Set apart for me [the Barnabas and Saul from your fellowship] for the work to which I have called them' (Acts 13:2). This confirmation provides tremendous moral support! It is one thing for your missionary to think the Lord has directed him. It is incredibly more reassuring to know He has confirmed it in the hearts of others as well.

Strategy Determined

The church fasted and prayed some more (Acts 13:3). Though Scripture isn't specific as to their prayers, it would seem logical that they were seeking guidance from the Lord for details of this new venture. The passage implies that a group larger than the two going heard answers to these questions: How should they go? Where is the money coming from? What do they take with them? When should they go? What are they going to do when they get there? Where is *there*? (See Matthew 10:1–16.)

This was a first as this team of senders determined how they could best be supportive to some of the Church's first missionaries. Remember, the Antioch church was filled with ordinary humans. Yet they were able to carry the weight of these unprecedented decisions as a team of people who had, in fasting and prayer, heard the Lord's direction. So can we today!

Commissioned

The senders laid their hands on the missionaries (Acts 13:3).

In Hebrews 6, the laying on of hands is named as one of the foundational doctrines. In this situation, the event was a commissioning, a setting-apart for a specific task, an identifying with the new ministry of the sent ones.

Whether your cross-cultural worker is going short-term or longer, he needs the spiritual covering – the moral support – of 'the laying on of hands,' because, as an extension of your church's ministry, he is going out to battle against the enemy.

Identifying with your missionary, of course, means that you'll need to do some fine-tuning of your understanding of what he'll be facing. You need to know what God is doing these days in cross-cultural outreach ministry. Become an expert on the steady progress of the twenty-first century's Great Commission endeavour.

Read how Jackie Pullinger broke through the Walled City of Hong Kong in *Chasing the Dragon*. Marvel at how a 19-year-old touched the lives of Latin American Indians in *Bruchko* by Bruce Olson. Weep in sorrow at the price Christ paid for the lost of Russia as you read *Vanya* by Myrna Grant or *Tortured For His Faith* by Haralan Popov.

Understand the cost of commitment in Pakistani Muslim Bilquis Sheikh's *I Dared to Call Him Father*. *Anointed for Burial* recounts God's work in Cambodia just before its fall. F. Kefa Sempangi gives a first person account of the martyrdom of Christians in Uganda in *A Distant Grief*. Rejoice that God has placed *Eternity in Their Hearts* as examined in Don Richardson's book on redemptive analogy, a key to proclaiming Christ to the nations. (See Resources, beginning on page 209 for information on obtaining these and other cutting-edge materials on today's mission to the world.)

As you identify with your missionary's work, what you learn about God's work around the world will bring a deeper sense of your part in God's global purpose and of how your role is critical as you give moral support to those who say, 'I believe the Lord wants me to go to the mission field! And I want you, church, to send me!'

A Case Study in Moral Support

More members of the sending team we met in Chapter One recount some of their experiences in learning how to offer their missionaries some solid moral support:

> Those of us who know Lou and Sandy personally would probably sum up our offers of moral support to them in these words: 'We love you and are here to help you in any way we can. We believe in the vision the Lord has given you to go to the Philippines. But in our eagerness to help you on your way, don't lose sight of the fact that we will greatly miss you.'
>
> After the core group – which is what we call the leadership of our Lou and Sandy support team – was established in June, things began to roll at seemingly breakneck speed. Looking back on it all now, we see that the moral support we gave was intertwined with our actions in all the other areas of support. When Lou and Sandy had to get out of their house and into temporary lodgings for a month before

leaving for training in Mexico, a home was graciously opened to them.

Have you ever prepared for a garage sale? Lou and Sandy had to go through everything they owned: Do we sell this? Store it? Take it with us? Ultimately the decisions were Lou and Sandy's, but to be nearby with a listening ear and an opinion was part of our moral support. The willingness of people to find boxes, store things safely, build a crate for shipment, advertise the sale, price everything and bring meals again and again after the pots and pans were packed expressed the moral support so needed and appreciated by Lou and Sandy.

Since they have left, we have found other ways to give moral support. On their last Sunday at church we had a large banner made which said, 'Bon voyage, Lou, Sandy and Marlies.' We later laid it out over several long tables and provided pens for people to write some words of encouragement. We sent the banner by boat so they would receive it after having been there for several months.

About six weeks after they left, baby Marlies had her first birthday. At our next core group meeting we had balloons, party hats, cake and ice cream – and kids. We sang 'Happy Birthday' to Marlies. We videoed the fun, and because we had time left on the tape, we took the camcorder to church on Sunday and had friends give Lou, Sandy and Marlies a special hello.

The enthusiasm and excitement that still accompanies any of the activities we arrange for our missionaries lets us know the moral support is running high. Though letter writing generally falls into the category of communication support, the fact that Lou and Sandy receive so many letters is most certainly a boost to their morale. In one six-week period, they reported they had gone only three days without receiving at least one letter, and one day they had received seven!

Moral support is obviously basic if you're serving as a sender. Maybe your forte as a sender will be boosting your missionary's morale. Do you always see the glass 'half full'? Can you easily put an encouraging word in an appropriate context? Do you think you can develop this skill?

But other areas of support are important too if your sent one is going to be fully supported. Somebody has to help with the nuts and bolts, the 'thousands' of details to be considered while your friend is preparing to go, while he is on the field and when he returns home. Missionaries need careful, solid *logistics* support.

(In addition to the individual study below, see the **Group Leader's Guide** for session two beginning on page 194.)

For Your Personal Involvement

- Read Matthew 12:20 from a number of translations. Choose one that really communicates the message to you. Memorize it. Meditate on it. Allow the Holy Spirit to infuse this concept of moral support deep into your being.
- Read, in its context, the story of each of the individuals in the Bible we referred to. Place next to their names the relationship of the people who could have been of moral support to them:

David, 1 Samuel 30 _____

Jesus, Luke 22 _____

Mary, Matthew 1 _____

The blind man, John 9 _____

Paul, Acts 21 _____

- Choose one of the stories. In your own words, retell the story as if those people had given moral support.
- Think of some advertising slogans that, if followed, could easily distract you from giving moral support to your missionaries. For example: 'When the going gets tough, the tough go shopping.'
- What are some biblical proverbs to govern our actions in moral support?

Action Steps

By the time you have read Chapter Two, completed the 'For Your Personal Involvement' section and participated in a discussion group, you should:

- Understand that moral support is the basic foundation of the support system.
- Be ready to express appreciation and give moral support to everyone in the fellowship who is a functioning part of the body.
- Realize that moral support is an ongoing relationship with your missionary.
- Write to one of your missionaries on the field and say, 'Here is my belated "Bon voyage!" God bless you!'
- Involve others. You might be surprised how contagious enthusiastic moral support becomes! Encourage others with the practice of encouragement!

Chapter Three

Logistics Support

*'When you come, bring the cloak that I left with Carpus at Troas,
and my scrolls, especially the parchments.'*
2 Timothy 4:13

'Sure, I had had some good training in building a support team. I had made provision for my logistics support. A very nice guy called Bill had said he would handle everything. Looking back, that should have been my first clue that it might not work out. Nobody can handle everything! But I didn't think of it at the time.

'A ministry opportunity had opened up. We had been invited to lead some relief work in the Middle East. We sensed God's direction in this. Things were coming together well. A lot of clothes and medicine were being given to us to distribute once we got there. We neatly packed and identified each box. Bill said that when sailors from our church came to a nearby military installation, he would get each of them to bring a few. Or he was sure he could arrange space for the whole shipment through diplomatic channels. What a relief to my mind. I could concentrate on other details.

44

'Three years later, we came home for a short visit. I sheepishly went to the friend who had let us store those boxes in his garage for these three years. Yep! They were all there! Just as we had left them! Not one had been sent to us.

'We shipped the stuff to a ministry in Mexico. They said they could use what wasn't outdated. I took the few remaining boxes of our personal items to Bill. "Yeah, sure! No problem. Those will be on the next ship out!"

'Well, we're ready to come home on furlough again. We've decided that since we've made it for six years over here without that stuff, we really don't need it. It will be interesting, though, when we get home to look through the boxes to see what one day had seemed so important to us.

'Bill's a good man. But he just didn't seem to be able to get those boxes over to us!'

Logistics support deals with handling the nuts and bolts of your cross-cultural worker's continuing home country responsibilities.

Logistics support must be considered on two levels: 1) Those areas of business to be attended to by the church leadership or missionary society and 2) the multitude of details that can be handled by a team of individuals. You, as part of the Logistics Support Team, could find yourself involved in:

- Identifying the cross-cultural workers in your fellowship.
- Maintaining accountability in ministry.
- Confirming and encouraging spiritual growth.
- Managing business affairs.
- Attending to personal details.

Identifying Cross-Cultural Workers

The local congregation, the body of Christ in microcosm, in order to function as a body, must have all the necessary parts. The body needs a mouth, so he appointed some prophets and pastor and teachers. The body needs to function 'decently and in order,' so he gave some the gift of administration.

He even has someone always 'just hanging around' like the appendix! And because outreach is one of the main functions of the Church, and because He said, 'The field is the world' (Matthew 13:38), God has placed in every body parts that are to minister cross-culturally.

In many churches, cross-cultural workers have not been given the opportunity to exercise their gifts, so they sit in atrophy, wondering, 'Why am I here?' They may try to find a place of ministry in some other area, but they just don't fit in! So in frustration they move from one ministry to another – or from one church to another.

The first logistical responsibility of the church, then, is to provide for the identification and exercise of the cross-cultural parts.

When Barnabas and Saul returned to Antioch from Jerusalem with some firsthand reports from the apostles, the church identified and put forth five men – prophets and teachers, leaders in the church. Then, in prayer and fasting, the church heard the Holy Spirit say, 'I want Barnabas and Saul for some cross-cultural work.' (A rather loose paraphrase of Acts 13:1–2!)

The local fellowship of believers must take the initiative in the missionary process by identifying the cross-cultural parts of the body and allowing them to exercise their gifts.

A missions fellowship at your church, then, becomes an ideal testing ground for potential missionaries. Under the direction of a lay or staff leader, those who believe they are your body's cross-cultural parts can experience all aspects of missions. They can be challenged to the task of cross-cultural outreach ministry by speakers and cultural studies and reports. They can practise the art of missionary support – moral, logistics and so on. They can exercise their gifts by ministering to people from overseas in your own home town. As potential goers are identified, they can actually go on a mini-mission or short-term experience. And the identified senders can serve as their senders!

The pastor, missions committee or fellowship should not be the last to know when one of the members from your church is getting involved in missions! Take the initiative: make cross-cultural outreach a part of the vision God has given you for your fellowship.

Maintaining Accountability In Ministry

Accountability has become one of the catchwords of our culture. And wouldn't we expect a reaction – at some time – to the 'do your own thing' philosophy? Yet, there are pastors and church leaders who do not know what those who have gone out from their church are doing. Some say, 'Well, they're with XYZ Society. Isn't that a good mission?'

Quite possibly. But . . .

Does that mission reflect the ministry goals of your church? Is that ministry targeting a decisive point of battle? Are your missionary's abilities and giftings suited to the work of that mission?

A second dimension of this responsibility then follows: once you are sure your cross-cultural worker is involved in a ministry suited to his gifts and the ministry thrust of your church, you must have some ongoing evaluation to know if that ministry is progressing. A regular, independent report from his supervisor will keep you in touch with his work.

If your missionary is working through a missionary society, make sure the lines of accountability are open, defined and include your fellowship. Remember, this missionary is still a part of your body.

One mission committee chair lamented, 'We sent them out to fulfil a responsibility that we knew they would do well. After a few months, the field leadership put the husband in another position for which he said he was not qualified. But he submitted. When he "really messed up", they sent him home "a failure."'

A report from your worker should keep you informed. A periodic phone call, an occasional report from another worker in the area – even a visit by someone from your church leadership would assure you that the ministry is really happening.

After all, the work of those who go and those who serve as senders is a team effort!

Confirming Spiritual Growth

Sadly, some sets of statistics report that for all their preparation, for all their 'hearing God's voice' and for all their support, up to 50 per cent of cross-cultural workers do not complete their first term of service.

Too many of them don't make it because of spiritual drought. They have dried up spiritually. They have come to the point where they are trying to give out more than they are taking in.

Church leadership must encourage spiritual growth 1) before missionaries go, 2) while they're on the field and 3) when they return home.

1) *Encouragement in spiritual growth before they go.*

Antioch provides a good example: Barnabas and Saul were mature leaders chosen by the Holy Spirit for a very tough assignment. It is easy to study their fine qualifications in Scripture.

For some reason, however, they took John Mark along. Evidently he was not prepared; when the going got tough, he quit!

Several years later, Paul sensed that John Mark still was not ready (Acts 15:38). But then several years after that assessment, Paul told Timothy to bring Mark with him, for 'he is helpful to me in my ministry' (2 Timothy 4:11).

A goer's eagerness to be sent doesn't necessarily mean he is ready to be sent.

One church does it this way: all those who even think they are cross-cultural parts of the body are encouraged to attend the missions fellowship headed by a cross-cultural coordinator. Here they are regularly exposed to cross-cultural outreach through prayer for the peoples of the world, speakers and videos of ministries and opportunities for ministry, including short-term awareness and ministry trips.

As a person (or couple) *and* the group sense the call of the potential goer, that person begins relating with the senior pastor in personal discipleship training. When he has functioned for a time in some position of leadership, he is ready for cultural training and developing a personal support team.

The church must send a capable, credible worker – one who knows what he believes and why. That confidence may come through in-house training, sending him to a Bible school or a combination of several preparation programmes.

The church must send those who have stripped the gospel and teachings of Christ of all British, Greek and Hebrew culture so that they can allow the host culture to clothe the gospel in a way suitable to them.

Senders must send one who has been trained in interpersonal relationships, the lack of which is the greatest reason for missionary dropouts! The church must not send one who is 'always learning but never able to acknowledge the truth' (2 Timothy 3:7), but one who is 'growing in the knowledge of God' (Colossians 1:10).

2) Encouragement in spiritual growth on the field.

Once a field worker becomes unencumbered with the affairs of his life at home (see 2 Timothy 2:4) and is thrust into the midst of endless opportunities for ministry, it is very easy for him to neglect his own spiritual intake – to be working so hard *for* the Lord that he neglects his personal relationship *with* the Lord. Soon yesterday's prayers, last week's Bible reading, last month's study of the Word of God are not able to sustain the worker through today's demands. And he falls prey to spiritual drought.

The writer of Hebrews says, 'By this time you ought to be teachers but you need someone to teach you . . . Let's not (lay) again the foundation . . . (but) go on to maturity' (Hebrews 5:12–6:3).

Because your worker doesn't have five Christian radio stations, two Christian TV stations and several Bible studies to choose from each week, he must be a student of the Bible – one who correctly handles the Word of Truth, a workman who does not need to be ashamed (2 Timothy 2:15). He must know how to feed himself spiritually.

You may help in this area perhaps by sending Bible study tapes to him, or by getting him to enrol on to a correspondence course. Perhaps you can study with him by letter or email on a book by book Bible study.

One missionary family in Peru arranged for their church to send weekly Bible study tapes. They soon began to listen to them in a group Bible study with other team members. Before long many groups were organized and listening! When they heard a few new choruses on the study tapes, they began to miss their Christian music. They quickly got on the radio to ask a support team member to send some Christian music tapes down – soon! Yes, some regions of the world are still not connected to the computer!

3) *Encouragement in spiritual growth when they come back home.*

Your missionary may come home for a brief stay before he returns to the field. Check his spiritual temperature. Many have been bombarded by new ideas and ideals, different values and beliefs. Are the changes in his thinking only cultural? Or has a subtle pantheism or other deceptive world system outlook permeated his doctrine? He may need a strengthening of his faith. More seriously, he may need a redefining of his Christian foundations. Some slightly askew winds of doctrine may even have come from the isolated team of the organization through which he is working.

You may also want to check what cultural artefacts your missionary brings home. As curious as they may be, if they have been used in demonic worship, they may carry unwelcome problems.

If your worker has come home to take up a new ministry here, you cannot assume that his spiritual growth will continue. Here at home he is bombarded by materialism and hedonism. These can have a drastic effect on his doctrine! Make sure he is still sharing what he 'first received from the Lord' (1 Corinthians 15:3).

A certain family served on a two-year mission assignment in the Far East. They returned home to resume ministry. It wasn't until much later – fifteen years later – through the counsel of their church leadership that they came to understand the intensity of the spiritual assault that had been launched against their whole family while overseas. They then began to work on breaking the powers of darkness and the resulting destructive patterns and began to live in the victorious freedom available in Christ. Supportive, intense prayer for them by the church when they first came home might have identified this problem sooner.

Managing Business Affairs

If your worker goes through a missionary society, most of the following issues will be established by the society's policy. Reading through some of these perplexing logistics might make you appreciate what a society goes through to keep missionaries overseas. Even if these tasks are handled by the society it is still your responsibility to know its policies and how you as the sending church relate to them. More and more missionary societies are asking for the church to be more actively involved in the whole missions process – including logistics.

If your church sends out missionaries directly to work with national ministries or to plant churches in unreached groups, think through each of the following issues first and plan carefully. And remember that the list is only a cursory look at the business matters that will come up!

1) *Money*

This one word conjures up more emotion than any other in the whole arena of missions! Because of its importance, someone in the church leadership must be responsible for handling the details.

a) Work with the national ministry and your cross-cultural worker to determine a necessary and adequate monthly budget.
b) Establish acceptable methods for securing enough financial support.
c) Record and communicate how each donor identifies his gift as designated for a particular missionary and/or project.
d) Develop a system for receipting the donor and for notifying your cross-cultural worker of amounts and who donated. Include the donor's address so his missionary can send a personal note of thanks. Careful financial monitoring is needed actually to transfer those funds overseas. Will any be kept back for administering the funding process? What will you do if donations fall below the established quota?

2) *Taxes*

How easily Jesus reduced to simplicity the whole issue of taxes (see Matthew 33:15–22). But earthly governments seem to be able to make things very complicated. Therefore 'rendering unto Caesar' requires an astute mind knowledgeable of the myriads of details involved. Details such as deductions, tax status changes caused by your worker being 'non-gainfully employed', length of residence outside the UK, the host country's tax system etc. are just the tip of the iceberg. If your fellowship does not have the time to keep up with all the laws, find a tax professional who can help with your missionary's situation before you send your worker to the field – just to make sure all is in order in this vital area of logistics support.

Mary was just going to Hong Kong for two years. 'I won't be earning any money in the United States. I don't need to worry about taxes!' she thought. She discovered how wrong she had been when, after returning home, she had to explain why she hadn't filed her income tax forms for two years. Back taxes plus interest meant that she had to make painful payments for several years.

Or take Sue, who thought that because her church had written a letter, she didn't have to pay Social Security. Don't let your cross-cultural worker become a horror story of trouble with the Inland Revenue.

3) Health

Responsible church leaders will make sure their cross-cultural worker and his whole family are in good health – physically, emotionally, mentally and spiritually – before they go to the field. Leaders must further see that their health care needs overseas are met in an appropriate way.

Three considerations: 1) Will the church's policy cover your missionary family when they are out of the country? 2) Is the cost of the premium higher than the cost of health care in the country to which they are going? 3) Is the health care provided to expatriates by the host nation's medical programme?

Definitely related to the health and well-being of your cross-cultural worker is his safety. What will you as a sending church do if your worker gets into trouble in his host culture? What if he is caught in the cross-fire of a civil disturbance? What if the government is over-thrown? What if your worker is kidnapped?

Has your missionary (and you) had training in crisis management? Even in such simple, practical measures called 'target-hardening'? The organization to contact is Crisis Consulting International, 9452 Telephone Road, 223 Ventura, CA 93004, USA. Phone: (805) 642-2549; Email: info@CriCon.org

The list goes on. Tragic are the stories of missionaries whose first thoughts about 'what to do' come as the bullets are shooting off the lock on their door!

Some hard facts. But it is far better to have these issues thought out ahead of time and to have a plan of action in place than to wait for your worker's phone call from prison to begin thinking about such matters!

4) Death

Death is an inevitable fact of life. Yet this most emotionally charged event is sometimes totally unplanned for by a missionary's sending church. To clarify the necessary details, your fellowship must plan ahead.

It is generally accepted that the best place to be buried is where the person dies. Many countries do not embalm; therefore they require burial within 24 hours.

The cost of immediate or even chartered flights out of a country is usually prohibitive. Furthermore, 'He lived, he worked, he died and he is buried among us,' is a powerful statement of the incarnation of Christ in your cross-cultural worker among a targeted people group. His testimony lives on!

A further emotionally charged consideration is the expense of a missionary coming home for the funeral of a relative. Do you tell your missionary that you simply can't afford to fly him home to comfort his mother at his father's funeral because you weren't prepared? Will you take up a special offering for such an emergency? Do you maintain an emergency fund?

Carefully think through these and other life-and-death policies.

Attending to Personal Details

Beyond this array of details that are best handled by the missionary society and church leaders under their spiritual and corporate covering, there is a host of bits and pieces of logistical matters that can be handled by an individual. The list here merely suggests the innumerable situations that could arise with your particular field worker.

1) Material goods

If their car didn't sell before they left, you could hold power of attorney to sell it for them – at agreed terms, of course. You could manage the rental or lease of their house. You could make payments from their bank account for property, insurance or other financial commitments. You could send them the proper income tax forms, licence-renewal forms, credentials or certificates. You could store the boxes of personal belongings which they chose not to sell or take with them. And, of course, you could arrange to send necessary materials to them – on time!

2) Family matters

You may be called upon to be executor of your missionary's will. You may be asked to be the guardians of their children if death should occur. You may be the ideal person to visit or care for their elderly parents. You may be able to provide a home for their university age child attending college in your town. You may have the contacts to provide the home-schooling curriculum materials they need. You may represent your missionary at family gatherings or events. Or, even care for their pet parrot while they are away!

3) Ministry needs

You could collect and post ministry items to your workers – Bibles, food and clothing for the poor, Sunday school materials and pictures. Since prices of many types of technical equipment are much lower in the UK; you could become your missionary's source for information and purchase of computers, modems, fax machines, hand-crank or solar-powered cassette, CD or DVD players. You might research and buy video and audio blank tapes, CDs and other supplies. Or you might put your goers in touch with sources so that they can purchase directly.

These jobs only suggest the size and diversity of this important support role. Selected members of your sending team with real gifts of service must attend to all your worker's responsibilities that continue in his home country. For, as Paul admonished Timothy, 'No man going to war entangles himself with the affairs of daily living' (2 Timothy 2:4). And there is no doubt that your friend is on the frontline of spiritual warfare.

Logistics support is essentially caring for each other in the body of Christ. The Bible teaches a simple doctrine: we really do need each other. We are the family of God, the body of Christ. Paul simply said that the body should work together as a whole with all the members having the same care one for another (1 Corinthians 12:25).

Logistics support members must have certain qualifications:

Diligence: Sometimes it takes a bit of research to find all
the correct income tax forms. Sometimes it takes some
creative looking to find an inexpensive source (or any
source) for New Testaments in the Uzbek language!

Concern for details: How to post items – completing the
customs forms, packaging, postage, labelling – takes time
and communication with the field worker regarding postal
requirements in the host country and detailed concern in
working with the UK Postal Service or other carrier. In the
UK, the P.O. produces a series of leaflets about how to send
parcels etc. abroad, with lists of destinations and surface –
and airmail charges. Many items can be sent in a jiffy bag
or at a 'small packet' rate. Customs forms and airmail
stickers are available at all post offices.

New missionaries in Peru got a notice from the Lima
post office that a parcel of homemade cookies had
arrived. When presented with an exorbitant import duty
for the shipment, the missionaries decided they should
pay it for the sake of their relationship with the well-
meaning senders . . . until an experienced missionary
told them the parcel would have been 'accidentally'
damaged and all the cookies would be gone anyway!
Logistics support must be concerned with details such as
import duties on parcels.

Punctuality: When you get a request for an item from
your cross-cultural worker, the chances are that a week or
two has already passed since the need became acute.
Finding what was requested, packing and sending it – in
addition to the return mail time – can cause quite a delay.
Any procrastination increases the wait.

Sound business practices: Your record-keeping and promptness of payment in your missionary's financial dealings is a reflection of their integrity in business.

One missionary family turned the management of the rental of their house over to a friend. Bills and receipts accompanied every cheque that this friend wrote. The records were kept with accuracy. The businesslike manner of their friend gave them confidence that all would be well when they returned.

Be assured that the peace of mind you as a good logistics support person can provide for a cross-cultural worker is equal in value to the things you do for him. What a privileged opportunity to serve as a sender!

Case Study in Logistics Support

The core group we have been following shows us more on this area of support:

> The logistics support we provide for Lou and Sandy includes legal aspects such as serving as executors and keepers of their wills. It also involves taking care of some of their financial affairs such as income tax and life insurance payments. It has even included selling their car.
>
> Lou and I were room-mates in college and have managed to remain close friends ever since. It was this long-standing relationship that led Lou to ask me to take care of his business while he and Sandy were in the Philippines. It seemed like a simple task: send an occasional cheque, file a form or two . . . It was – I thought – no big deal!
>
> As Lou and Sandy prepared to go to a training course in Mexico, they were very busy and we never seemed to find the time to get together. We finally found one half-hour to discuss how they ran their lives, what bills they had due

each month and how we were going to handle their financial affairs. Additionally, we met at their bank to make me a signatory on their savings account and to complete a power of attorney form that authorized me to have full control of their business affairs.

As I started paying their bills, I quickly realized that I needed a system to keep records of what I had paid. Thankfully my wife is much more organized than I and produced an old bill-organizer that is working fine. It will hopefully provide them with a full account of what we have done when they return from the Philippines.

Taking over their financial affairs hasn't been easy. There have been those unexplained bills – like the demand from a life insurance company. Do I pay this? I didn't know how to handle this one!

Then there was the car! 'The Bomb,' as Lou affectionately called it, was one of those things that gives used car salesmen such a bad reputation. Suddenly I found myself faced with having to sell a car I wouldn't wish on my worst enemy! Fortunately, a mechanic friend of Lou's was willing to take it as a 'project' car.

The hardest part of what we are doing is the realization that we could really mess up someone else's business credibility, and that they are not in a position to do anything about it. It came to a head when we needed to find out if they wanted us to do their tax return or send all the information to them. As the deadline approached, we realized that the post would not go back and forth fast enough to communicate.

We checked with the phone company and found the cheapest times to call that would still fit into both our schedules. After trying to connect for half an hour, we prayed that if the decision we had come to about their taxes was wrong, we would get through the next time. The next time, Lou answered the phone! We had made the wrong decision and were able to straighten out a number of nagging questions. Our peace of mind – and theirs as well – cost very little.

The lessons we logistics supporters have already learned about how to do this right include:

1) Sit down for several sessions with the couple you are sending. Even if they are going out with a well-known missionary society or association, don't assume that all their personal business matters will somehow be taken care of. Go over taxes, past and present. Discuss every financial obligation they have. Find out why they have these bills and why they pay them the way they do and whom to contact when questions arise.

2) Get a full power of attorney for the husband and wife separately.

3) Set up a record-keeping system with the couple before they leave. Find out how they want their records maintained so that you don't just hand them a stack of old bills and cancelled cheques when they return.

4) Make sure that their wills are complete and on file with their executor. If that is you, get a safe deposit box. Make sure they have expressed how they wish their remains to be disposed of. Lou, being a very practical guy said, 'The cheapest way possible!'

5) Pray about the responsibility you are about to accept. The enemy just loves to confuse and condemn anyone trying to do anything for the Lord – even something as simple as paying a few bills!

This is logistics support at its best! There is no way of anticipating what your missionary will ask for; there is no knowing when a request will come. But one committed to the task and diligent in the work is a rare and prized partner in cross-cultural ministry. You may just be that person.

But for your missionary to sense the full support he needs, other areas of your possible service become important also. So that he may become 'disentangled with the affairs of this life' and preach the gospel freely, those who provide the *financial* support become a vital part of the team.

(In addition to the individual study below, see the **Group Leader's Guide** for session three beginning on page 196.)

For Your Personal Involvement

- Read Paul's account of co-operation in the body of Christ from 1 Corinthians 12. Particularly note the care given to the 'unpresentable' parts.
- In the book of Acts, underline all references to travel logistics. With today's electronic communication systems, how could someone 'back home' have helped in each of these instances?
- Make a list of all the things in your life that would need attention 'back home' if you went away for two years. These are probably the things your missionary has to find someone to handle when he leaves.

Action Steps

By the time you have read Chapter Three, completed the 'For Your Personal Involvement' section and participated in a group discussion, you should:

- Understand the potentially vast number of details involved in logistics support.
- Be more aware that we are the body of Christ and we really do need each other.

- Decide whether God wants you to be on the Logistics Support Team of a cross-cultural worker you know. If so, write to him and inquire about any logistical needs that he may have. Make yourself available to assist in that need.
- Involve others. As you come to understand the value of this type of support, encourage others to consider it as their place in the body of Christ.

Chapter Four

Financial Support

*'I rejoice greatly in the Lord that at last you have renewed your
concern for me. Indeed, you have been concerned, but you had no
opportunity to show it. I am not saying this because I am in need,
for I have learned to be content whatever the circumstances.
I know what it is to be in need, and I know what it is to have plenty.
I have learned the secret of being content in any and every situation,
whether well fed or hungry, whether living in plenty or in want.'*
Philippians 4:10–12

'In totally miraculous ways God opened four major doors
to bring us to Cameroon, West Africa, as Short-Term
Assistants (STAs) with Wycliffe.

'Being STAs wasn't new to us. We had spent two
eventful years in Mexico and later thought of serving
again – sometime. But I had no idea returning to the field
was the reason for an appointment at 8 a.m. one
September morning with Wycliffe's Superintendent of
Children's Education.

'But the longer we talked, the more I wondered if God
wanted us on the field again – now! By 9:30 a.m. we
decided I wasn't the one to go to Nepal; by 10:30 I had

some reservations about Papua New Guinea; by 11:00 we were praying for God's direction for me to be a principal-teacher in Cameroon.

'"We're going to Africa!" I announced as I walked through the front door of our home that day. While my wife Jill and I prayerfully considered the decision, we knew God would have to open several doors which could keep us from going if they remained closed.

'The first one was to do with our oldest son James, who was only a semester away from graduation. Would it even be fair to him to change schools again? Though we definitely wanted him to go with us, it would have to be his decision. As days merged into weeks, his attitude changed from "Do your own thing, but don't expect me to go" to "Let's get going!"

'Our home represented another obstacle. How could we ever find a family to be totally responsible for the house for two years? But in God's time scale He brought close friends to Southern California for a furlough from their ministry with Wycliffe in Mexico. They moved in – we moved out, leaving pictures on the walls and sheets in the airing cupboard.

'A third problem was my mother-in-law's health. She was battling with cancer and really depending on Jill for moral support. God took care of her needs through a miraculous healing!

'The fourth door to be opened had dollar signs on it! We learned that the cost of living in Cameroon was as high as in Southern California. We sent a letter to our friends – those who we thought would be interested in what we felt sure God wanted us to do. Money began coming in. A bonus on the job. A buyer for the car and caravan. Our church had just decided to double its support for Wycliffe families. Friends pledged towards our monthly needs.

'We received official approval from the Wycliffe Board. Passports and immunizations were now in order. We were assured our visas would arrive between the 12th and 15th of November. We set our departure date: 10 p.m. on the 18th of November from the Los Angeles airport.

'All the normal hectic things were happening: we were trying to buy lightweight clothing in winter; packing, weighing, repacking; finding a mislaid birth certificate; sending out another letter; having the last gala round of visits with friends.

'Then 18th of November came. At 8 a.m. I was making the final tally of our financial situation – a task I had intentionally delayed. I just couldn't make it all add up. We were $50 a month short.

'"I just cannot sign our Statement of Financial Preparedness," I regretfully told Jill. We all laughed at the ridiculousness of our situation. Luggage filled the living room. The kids had officially left school. Our car was sold. Our friends were already living with us – and wanted us to get out of *their* house! All goodbyes had been said. We were holding thousands of dollars of non-redeemable airline tickets in our hands. We'd radioed Africa that we were on our way. And here we were $50 a month short of our support goal!

'"The Lord must be planning to send in some money today," I said as I put the statement aside, unsigned.

'At 9 a.m. Jill's mother called, asking if we needed any money. She then related an incredible story about Myrna, a lady in their church. She had been on our financial support team during our time with Wycliffe in Mexico. And she had heard us present the financial needs for this new venture in Cameroon. Unbeknown to us, she had been struggling for several weeks to find a way in which God could use her again on our financial support team.

'But it was now the night before we were to leave. Myrna spent a sleepless vigil asking the Lord for some way that she could still help us. Their business was in financial difficulties and their house had just been burgled. At 4 a.m. she dozed off and at 7 a.m. was up preparing to go to a church missions meeting. At 8 a.m. (while I was adding up) she put on a coat she hadn't worn since the previous winter. She put her hand in the pocket and, to her amazement, drew out $1200 in cash! The thief who had so thoroughly gone through her husband's clothing in that wardrobe three nights before had completely missed her coat!

'"This is for the Coopers!" she shouted. "Thank you, Lord for your faithfulness!"

'I said, "Praise the Lord!" The $1200 she found in the pocket and wanted us to have was exactly the $50 support for 24 months that we lacked. I ran for the Statement of Financial Preparedness and signed, "Yes, we are ready to go!"'

Financial support is the most controversial and so the most talked-about of the six areas of support. In fact when you mention missionary support, most people think of nothing else but money.

As Christians we must steer a course between two extremes. On the one hand, we are made to feel guilty by the millions who are starving to death because we do not give £5 to such-and-such an organization. At the other extreme, we are told 'Prosperity is your divine right!' Where do we turn for balance in financial responsibility?

To further complicate the issue is the problem of materialism in the West. The media create and then cash in on society's poor self-image by saying, 'You aren't good enough ... until you use our product!' So we toil endlessly to purchase this and that, only to find out in the next commercial that a 'new and improved' version is now available. As the bumper sticker says, 'I owe, I owe, so off to work I go!' How do we rise above the trivia of this world to see financial responsibility from God's perspective?

His Word, of course, communicates His perspective. On the stub of every pay cheque received by Christians could be the words of Deuteronomy 8:18: 'Remember the LORD your God, for it is He who gives you the ability to produce wealth.' Why does God bless us with wealth?

God's principle that His people are blessed to be a blessing is established in the covenant He made with Abraham (see Genesis 12).

Some ways of raising money to bless the world through cross-cultural outreach ministry include cake sales and car washes, paper and can recycling. And in an increasingly waste-conscious economy, these endeavours do generate some working capital. A garage sale with all or a portion of the proceeds going to a missions project or missionary can bring families together for good causes. Art and craft items can be made and sold and the profit given to a missionary. God blesses us with ingenuity, mouth-watering recipes and entrepreneurial skills so that financially we can bless the spread of His Kingdom.

But the time will come when all garages are clean, people will want to keep their remaining newspapers to light winter fires, and everybody has had their fill of fundraising pizzas.

More likely, the time will come when your cross-cultural outreach ministry has grown beyond the funds that can be generated by these methods. And now diligent effort must be made to look beyond these efforts to more creative, long-lasting ways of raising money for cross-cultural outreach ministry. Let's look at three areas of biblical stewardship: giving, lifestyle and managing wealth.

Giving

We know the Word: 'God loves a cheerful giver.' 'It is more blessed to give than to receive.' 'Give, and it shall be given to you. When you give . . .' Yet the brilliance of the Bible's simple teaching on the principle of giving invariably comes round to 'how much?' which inevitably leads to tithing, which ultimately deals with the nitty-gritty of, 'Do I tithe on my net or on my gross income?' And we have run into the same dead end as the Jews to whom Jesus said, 'You give a tenth of your spices – mint, dill and cummin. But you have neglected the more important matters of the law . . . You strain out a gnat but swallow a camel' (Mathew 23:23–24).

The discipline of tithing (which Jesus commended the Jews for doing) leads a Christian to a deeper commitment of 'cheerful' giving (2 Corinthians 9:7) which grows into the willing mind principle of 2 Corinthians 8:12–14: 'That there might be equality!'

Using this principle, as long as we compare ourselves only to those wealthier than we are, we don't feel too compelled to give. But when we enlarge our vision to encompass the world, the principle of equality has us giving and giving some more since the 'poverty' level in the West is equivalent to great wealth in most Two-Thirds World countries. We are indeed rich.

A well-known hymn says: 'I surrender all, I surrender all. All to Jesus I surrender; I surrender all.' May we, in our responsible stewardship of finances, grapple with God's Word and the work of the Holy Spirit in our lives, to that point of full surrender.

Before we go on, let's look again at the basic concept: if every Christian in your fellowship tithed, that tithe would keep the treasurer busy each week trying to decide how to spend it. We must recognize, however, that a 'tithe' means 10 per cent. As we have moved into the twenty-first century, statistics show that all charitable giving amounted to 2.7 per cent!

None of us likes to hear a 20-minute sermon on giving before each offering is taken. But the very concept of 'taking' an offering instead of 'Freely you have received, freely give' (Matthew 10:8) might be educating us to be miserly in our giving. Sometimes even the prayer said at offering time does more to support our meagre giving than to encourage a 'generous, cheerful, hilarious' free-will gift: 'Father, you know we only have these few pennies to give to you. But you multiply them so the whole world can believe in you!' And we put away our wallets and pull out our loose change – if we have any!

Or we are taught to 'pay' our tithes. As with any other bill, therefore, a conscious or unconscious resentment can develop. Rather, the Bible urges that God's people 'bring all the tithes into the storehouse' (Malachi 3:10). 'Lay up for yourselves treasures in heaven, where moth and rust don't destroy' (Matthew 6:20). That sounds more like securing a sound investment than 'paying a bill'. And that grows into, 'What a privilege that God would allow me to be part of His Plan of the Ages. He could get along without my money, for "He owns the cattle on a thousand hills" (Psalm 50:10). But the Lord is giving me an opportunity to invest in His Kingdom!'

Giving is an act of intelligent worship. 'Let every man who will do it willingly from his heart bring me an offering' (Exodus 25:2). 'Every man shall give as he is able' (Deuteronomy 16:17). 'The disciples, each according to his ability, decided to provide help for the brothers living in Judea' (Acts 11:29). 'But first there must be a willing mind' (2 Corinthians 8:12). 'Each man should give what he has decided in his heart to give' (2 Corinthians 9:7).

What do we learn from His Word? That generous, cheerful, hilarious giving is not an awkward interruption to worship, but the very essence of it.

How can we be wise about our giving?

Unfortunately, not all individuals and organizations vying for your support are themselves wise stewards. There are three questions you must ask to check them on their accountability:

1) *Is the money you give going where they say?* Do they take 60p of your pound to raise additional funds? A dedicated sender once gave a very large donation to an international project. A year later, those who had solicited this gift came back to him, apologizing that they had not used the money as they had told him. Would he forgive them? Did he want his money back? An apology doesn't happen often! The funds are more likely to be hidden in the language of the book-keeper's report!
2) *Is the project or missionary service really hitting a decisive point in the battle for souls?* God wants us to be a part of ministries that yield 'fruit that will last' (John 15:16).

    You might even have to say 'no' to your closest friend's appeal if you sense his 'summer of service' sounds more like a sun and surf holiday!

    Worthwhile missionary service is as diverse as the creative genius of God flowing through His obedient servants. And some of the activities seem way out there – somewhere! But if they are really hitting a decisive point in the battle for the souls of mankind, there will be a line of correlation that can be traced to 'fruit that will last.'

3) *If your cross-cultural worker is going out through a UK-based organization, what is the UK administrative/field use ratio of the mission's funds?* That is, how much is spent in the UK to get one pound to the field? Is it under 20 per cent? Are the UK personnel living on a comparable level to their field workers? How do they raise money? (By the way, if an organization doesn't want to answer this type of question, you have a pretty good idea of its accountability already!) God owns all; yet He is the most frugal economist!

Lifestyle

Statistics can bore or shock or motivate. For example: Americans spend as much on chewing gum in a year as they give to missions, and pay as much for pet food in 52 days as they spend annually on missions. Does our lifestyle, as Jesus said, tell us where our heart is? (Read Luke 12:13–24.)

The 'Queen Mary' was designed as a luxury liner, yet during World War II it was converted to serve as a troop carrier. Today the museum aboard the 'Queen Mary' affords a stunning contrast between the respective lifestyles in peace and war. On one side of a partition, the tables prepared for high society hold a dazzling array of dishes, crystal and silver. On the other side, one metal tray with indentations replaces 15 dishes and saucers. Bunks eight tiers high, accommodate 15,000 troops in contrast to 3,000 wealthy patrons in peacetime transport. To reconstruct the vessel so drastically took a national emergency. The survival of a nation depended upon it. Should you replace your china with metal trays? No! But allow the Holy Spirit to challenge every aspect of your lifestyle.

Our master calls out 'Rescue the perishing!' The captain of the Lord of Hosts has trumpeted a certain sound for battle. But the cry of the perishing is often lost in the din of self-survival. While pursuing comfort we can easily ignore Christ's warning in Scripture, 'Whoever tries to keep his life will lose it' (Luke 17:33). We deplore the diseases of the underdeveloped nations: tuberculosis, malnutrition, parasites, typhoid and others. Yet the West has virtually invented a whole new set of affluence-related diseases: obesity, arteriosclerosis, heart disease, strokes, lung cancer, cirrhosis of the liver and more. In saving ourselves we are well on our way to losing ourselves!

Any good cross-cultural training teaches the missionary to adapt as much as possible to the lifestyle of those he is going to minister among – a simpler lifestyle, a lower consumption of goods, a 'make-do and mend' attitude. This forms a solid principle of bonding – establishing a sense of belonging with those he serves.

Those who serve as senders might experience a new sense of belonging and a new vision of their part in rescuing the perishing if they, too, would adopt a lifestyle that approximates to that of those they are sending. Senders who take on this challenge often find that their *quality* of life improves.

A diligent Financial Support Team member must allow the radical challenges of these statements to question his lifestyle:

1) If I run out of money before the month runs out of days, a humbling but good starting point might be for me to ask for help in personal financial management.
2) If I look into a large wardrobe of clothes and don't see 'a thing to wear,' a new reading of 'do not worry about . . . what you will wear. Life is more than food

and the body more than clothes' (Luke 12:22–23) might give me a new perspective on the situation.

3) If my lifestyle demands a status symbol for transportation (or possession of anything for the purpose of making others envious), I should check carefully Christ's parable regarding taking the seat of honour in Luke 14:7–14.

4) If I dream about a house with long hallways and huge bedrooms and bathrooms for each family member, it might be worth me considering my Christian longings for a home in the city 'whose builder and maker is God' (Hebrews 11:10).

5) If my lifestyle roller-coasts on thrills and frills, it might be well for me to reduce the speed and turn down the volume enough to notice that life is ready to give free excitement and exhilaration through natural beauty (Psalm 19:1–3), fellowship (Acts 2:42) and worship (Psalm 34:1–4).

As we prayerfully consider the Holy Spirit's dealings in our lives we will yield to His Will. For 'He who began a good work in you will carry it on to completion' (Philippians 1:6; also see Philippians 2:12 and 13).

God's instructions about money are not 'one-size-fits-all.' There is no hint that Jesus ever told Mary, Martha and Lazarus to dispose of any of their wealth. And the record suggests they were quite well-to-do. Yet to the rich young ruler, He said, 'Sell your possessions' (Matthew 19:21).

Although many Christian books only make us feel guilty or tell us to tighten our belts, an excellent book on this subject is *Living More With Less* by Doris Janzen Longacre (see Resources, page 214). It contains hundreds of practical lifestyle changes that encompass every aspect of finance.

Christians with a renewed lifestyle can free up thousands of creative pounds for cross-cultural ministry. Living more with less is an exciting, viable option.

Managing Wealth

Just a cursory glance at the parable of the talents (Matthew 25:14–30) assures us that the Lord expects us to be wise in managing the wealth He has entrusted to us. In a related parable in Luke 19:11–27, He tells us to 'Put this money to work until I come back.'

We can exercise Christian stewardship on two levels: financial practices overseas and financial resources behind the lines.

Financial Practices on the Battlefield

- Missionaries could implement plans that include short-term, itinerant, Pauline-style assignments instead of strategies that demand costly land or property or other long-term investment. Admittedly, some cross-cultural assignments require a very long commitment – Bible translation, for one. But many mission assignments could be given to nationals sooner than they are, allowing your missionary to move on to new areas of need. A sad but valid criticism is that many jobs still being done by missionaries could be handled more effectively by nationals! Notice Paul's strong encouragement to Titus to 'appoint elders in every city' (see Titus 1:5). His further note, quoting Crete's own prophet, suggests Titus was having a hard time finding qualified men – but he was to get on with it! (Titus 1:12).
- Another practice of biblical times was to move (for one reason or another) to a new area, become a resident of

that country and seek employment (see Acts 18:1–19 for the example of Aquila and Priscilla). In some situations your missionary could do this and release his funds for others.

- Making a greater use of tentmaker opportunities gets your missionary living and working with the people. Teaching English as a second language is one of the best opportunities; becoming an international student is a close second. But beyond these are thousands of jobs around the world that would allow your missionary to get *Out of the Saltshaker and Into the World* as a book by Rebecca Pippert challenges. There are some serious considerations, however, that must be given to this type of ministry. Don Hamilton's book *Tentmakers Speak Out* is particularly helpful reading in this area (see Resources, page 211).

- Self-support by independently wealthy or retired people is becoming a more viable option. With our increasing senior citizen population, agencies are specifically recruiting these people. The Finisher's Project is leading the way in this endeavour to challenge those who have taken early retirement to give this next phase of their life to cross-cultural ministry service (www.finishers.org).

- Living *among* the people instead of in guarded, gated communities in the suburbs may free needed funds. Paul reminded the elders of Ephesus, 'You know ever since I first came to Asia, how I have lived among you' (Acts 20:18). About Jesus, John wrote, 'The Word was made flesh and dwelled among us' (John 1:14). Jesus was a powerful example of living with the people. And later He said, 'As the Father sent me, I am sending you' (John 20:21).

- God, in His sovereignty has raised up a 'new wave' of missionary thrust, and it is coming from Two-Thirds

World nations themselves. Missionaries from the West can work with this move from God! 'Fruit that remains' is our goal. How can we most effectively co-operate with this Divine Plan? Paul, the great missionary statesman of the first century serves as an excellent model – again!

He was an evangelist. Most often we read of his preaching the gospel. (There were only a few exceptions – the most notable being his several years teaching in Ephesus). However, he did have a team of teachers (Timothy and Titus are the best known, but there were many others – see Acts 20:4) who were left behind to find faithful nationals and teach them the Word in such a way that they would go out and teach others (2 Timothy 2:2).

If you are in a position to formulate policy or financially support missionaries, be a wise and faithful steward. Study and network with mission strategists about wise financial policies. Don't establish a ministry that will forever be dependent on Western money. We should not teach methods of evangelism and discipling which require equipment inaccessible in the local situation – projectors, big buildings, expensive books, vehicles, etc. Let the simplicity of the gospel be clothed in the cultural garb of national people.

There are additional ways of maximizing funds for overseas ministries, by careful management of the wealth God has entrusted to us back home.

Financial resources behind the lines

Tax-Efficient Giving
There are now several ways in which the UK Government promotes and enhances our giving to established charities:

Gift Aid

Gift Aid is available to ordinary church members, not just
to business people and those who make written annual tax
returns. It enables the donor to increase the value of their
donations to charity by up to 28 per cent. The beneficiary
must be a *bona fide* charitable organization. You cannot
give by gift aid to an individual nor in any way which
results in monetary benefit to an individual. (There have
been some problems of late regarding the personalized
support of missionary personnel, where such funds are not
pooled. Societies affected will be able to advise you.)

The charity will reclaim the tax from the Inland
Revenue and add it to your gift.

The rules are:

1. A Gift Aid declaration form must be signed by an
   individual – this scheme is not open to churches and
   groups.
2. You must pay an amount of income tax and/or capital
   gains tax at least equal to the tax that the charity
   reclaims on your donations in the tax year (currently
   22p for each £1 you give). Not all of us do, but it
   should be remembered that those who live largely off
   savings and investments will probably be receiving
   their interest net of tax. If that is so, whether you
   realize it or not, to that extent at least you are a tax
   payer. There is no minimum sum although the
   associated paperwork probably means that gifts
   should be for at least £10 a year. Anything less is not
   cost effective. The maximum you may give is
   determined only by the amount of tax you actually
   pay. Payments can be large or small, regular or one-off,
   and can be made by regular monthly, quarterly or half-
   yearly installments if you prefer.

3. You can cancel this declaration at any time by notifying the charity. Christian charities will readily free you from your obligation on request.

4. If in the future your circumstances change and you no longer pay tax on your income and capital gains equal to the tax that the charity reclaims, you can cancel your declaration. Should your income in any year during the period in which you are making payments inadvertently fall below taxable level, you should simply advise the beneficiaries that you have no tax to pay that year and they will not claim the rebate.

5. If you pay tax at the higher rate you can claim further tax relief in your Self Assessment tax return.

6. Your executors face no obligations with regard to it after your decease.

7. If you are unsure whether your donations qualify for gift aid relief, ask the charity or ask your local tax office for leaflet 'IR113 Gift Aid'.

NB. In the case of those who covenant when paying tax only at the lower rate of 20 per cent, the Inspector, who will be making a rebate at 22 per cent, would be entitled to claim from the donor the small difference. In practice he is unlikely to do so except in the case of sizeable covenants.

The benefits to the Lord's work are evident. At the basic tax rate of 22 per cent the figures are as follows:

A gift of £100 becomes £128
A gift of £250 becomes £320
A gift of £500 becomes £641
A gift of £1,000 becomes £1,282

So a society whose donors covenant collectively £100,000 per year, will receive a tax rebate of £28,205!

The curious may well ask how it is that 22 per cent of £100 becomes £28. The answer is that in effect you are giving to the charity £128 of your already taxed salary and the tax you have paid on that part of your salary is added to your gift. Twenty-two per cent of £128 is £28. So you give the net sum of £100, and the £28 tax already paid on £128 of your income is handed on to the charity by the Inspector, making a total of £128.

For higher rate tax payers there is the further incentive that the difference between basic and higher rate tax levels is deductible from their next tax bill. This means that – with tax bands at 22 per cent and 40 per cent – for a charity to receive a benefit of £10,000, the actual cost to a higher rate tax payer will be no more than £6,500. The gift aid declaration would be for £6,750 net, the Inspector would add £1,900 to the charity and return £1,500 to the donor!

There are some Christians in the UK who oppose giving under this scheme on the grounds that the Church should not allow itself to become dependent on 'Caesar's' money. This argument, with respect, arises from a misconception. As has been shown above, the Government is not adding 'secular funding' to your gift. It is simply adding the tax you have already paid but which the law does not demand of you. It is therefore, properly understood, wholly *your* money which the charity receives, not some of yours and some of the Government's.

Gift Aid Made Easy

Some donors have more reasonable objections. They do not wish to commit themselves to the same sum every year for the same cause. But nowadays this problem is readily overcome by the use of a charity account.

Trusts which provide this service – there are several – accept payments in their favour for the sum(s) you wish to give to the Lord's work each year. The tax is reclaimed for you and added to an account from which you can disburse your giving in various ways as often or as seldom as you like, and for sums as large or small as you like. Your account will be charged with a small percentage to cover administrative costs, but the result is eminently beneficial. A £500 covenant with such a trust might look like this after the first year of operation

	£ OUT	£ IN	£ BALANCE
COVENANT GIFT			
Received for year one		500	500
Distribution to			
Bethany Baptist	200		300
Tax rebate added		141	441
Distribution to			
Asian Mission	50		391
Distribution			
for Bibles for the Blind	100		291
Distribution to			
Evangelistic Campaign	25		266
Charge for year			
2% of gross sum	13		253
DISTRIBUTION to			
XYZ project	200		53

In this example, your £500 has already produced gifts of £575 and a balance of £53 is still available to give away next year!

Disbursements are made either by asking the trust to send a cheque to the mission of your choice or by sending yourself direct a donation voucher (like a cheque) from the supply that they will provide you with. A reminder will arrive each year when your annual covenanted donation is due. The flexibility is enormously advantageous and the system much to be recommended.

Payroll Giving

Some sizeable employers are able to deduct gifts regularly from staff wages *before deduction of tax*, for forwarding to the charity specified by the employee. There is a stipulated maximum monthly deduction, the level of which will be modified from time to time. The personnel department will be able to tell you if such a scheme is available at your workplace.

Pound-For-Pound Schemes

Employees of large organizations, such as banks and multi-national companies, may find that their employers give annual donations to charity. Some have set up their own trusts in order to do so, others have introduced 'pound-for-pound' (or 'matching-gift' schemes) by which they pledge to double whatever gifts their employees make to charity, the employee specifying the beneficiary. Sadly, some employers do not allow religious organizations to benefit from such a scheme, even if registered as a charity. But there can be no harm in enquiring!

Making a Will

There are many reasons why we should make a will; not least for Christians is the fact that it gives us the right to determine what should happen to the resources God has entrusted to us after we have no further use for them.

Wills are often drawn up many years before their provisions become reality, and it is found that inflation has greatly reduced the original intention of the deceased. This can be readily avoided by dividing your estate into percentage shares and earmarking a determined number for the charities of your choice. As the total estate grows, so do the individual shares.

Bequests to the Lord's work in church and mission are free of inheritance tax, so making a careful will can limit the liability of your estate to such tax, and perhaps free it altogether. Making a will – and keeping it up to date – probably warrants legal advice, but there are many books and leaflets you can consult to help you with this essential and altogether worthwhile task. Most missions can guide you and have suitable clauses available for your use if you wish to leave them a bequest.

Fund Raising through Sponsorship Activity

There can be few in Britain who have not been asked by young people to sponsor them for this or that charitable activity. Cycle rides, half-marathons, swims, fell-walks, parachute jumps, 'readathons', sponsored silences – these and a hundred others have become methods by which young people raise money for good causes. Helping one young member of your congregation to raise enough to spend six weeks on the mission field of Africa or South America as a volunteer worker may seem to some an expensive way of giving a youngster a memorable experience, but it can well issue in a life-long dedication to Christian mission. Congregations, both at home and in the Two-Thirds World, have been spiritually renewed in a remarkable way by a carefully planned visit from a short-term volunteer team. It may seem to some to be light-hearted giving and light-hearted going, but in hundreds of cases during the past ten years, it has borne invaluable fruit for Christ.

Gifts in Kind

Christians in the United States, share excess goods by letting others buy them in so-called 'Thrift Stores'. These are usually stocked entirely by nearly-new goods gifted by Christians and operated by Christian volunteers, though a paid manager has sometimes proved cost-effective. The nearest equivalent in the UK would be our local charity shops which raise enormous sums for a variety of secular charities. There might be room, in a suitable local area, for someone in the UK to develop a similar operation which would dedicate its income to Christian mission.

A highly effective variation on this theme is already working in the UK, namely the Missionary Auctions. The money made from auctioning jewellery, silver or plated items, paintings, clocks, various antiques, general bric-a-brac, etc. is dedicated entirely to Christian outreach at home and abroad. Many of the gifts have been dug out by Christians across the country from all-but-forgotten corners in lofts and garages; some are unwanted and even unopened gifts! Teams of Christian professionals – valuers and auctioneers – give their time and expertise to make this a highly efficient and trustworthy service.

Churches and other groups can unite their efforts to produce various lots for the next auction. Donors are at liberty to specify the charity they want to benefit from the proceeds of their auctioned gift. Matthew 6:19 says: 'Do not store up for yourselves treasures on earth, where moth and rust destroy and where thieves break in and steal.' Surely as Christians in this country, often entrusted with more things of value than we can reasonably make use of, it is poor stewardship indeed to let them rust and deteriorate when they can be put to the cause of funding overseas workers, or sending study Bibles to pastors in deprived areas of the world.

Shop for the Kingdom

Online shopping is taking off, and just like regular shopping we're still faced with the usual consumer ethical choices but in a far bigger 'supermarket'. Many online stores run affiliate schemes and some are beginning to make contributions to a customer selected charity with each purchase. This is one way that you can help your favourite mission charity or project without it costing you a penny extra. At the forefront of this rapidly growing 'virtual marketplace' is Ebay.

Ebay recently launched 'Ebay for Charities', a scheme whereby anyone can auction something and give a percentage of the proceeds to charity. For more examples of shopping affiliate schemes, see www.oscar.org.uk.

Interest-Free Loans

Many UK Christian organizations are obliged to finance their operations with only the smallest of financial reserves. Inadequate cash-flow, especially where monies are subject to delay in international transmission, can prove restricting to the cause of Christ and considerably worrying to missionary executives who have overseas staff to feed. Interest-free loans from their supporters are usually a most welcome proposal. If you need to keep your capital for later use, but would be willing to loan it meantime to the Lord's work – and forego the interest on it – write and ask the society in question if they would be interested in such a loan and under what terms it could be repaid. You may wish – though it would certainly not be essential – to specify that such a loan would become an outright gift to the charity in the case of your decease.

The United Kingdom Evangelization Trust will accept such interest-free deposits, the money being totally secured and available for return to the depositor on demand. You may designate the charity to which you wish the resulting tax-free interest to go.

Christian fund-raising projects such as the highly successful Christmas Cracker, need considerable capital up-front to get their events off the ground, and may well be glad to return your money immediately afterwards with interest – as long as the whole amount is then dedicated to a predetermined charitable project.

And then, when your own giving is done, it should not be forgotten that there are a number of:

Grant Making Trusts

If you have in mind a specific project which requires funding, another source of money is available from the estates of Christian philanthropists who have left behind trusts to finance specific areas of endeavour. It is essential to read carefully the parameters which each trust has set for itself, and not waste trustees' time with applications wrongly or inadequately directed. These are found in the *Directory of Grant Making Trusts,* a copy of which can be found in most local reference libraries. A visit could prove extremely worthwhile.

Investing for the Lord

It is not known what markets the stewards traded in in The Parable of the Talents, but it is unlikely that they just 'put it in the bank'. Even at 10 per cent interest the master must have gone on a very long journey to double the money. The unfaithful steward was reprimanded for not doubling his! (See Matthew 25:14–30.) Churches in the United States often pool the personal resources of their members so that the investment of 'mutual funds' can bring higher returns for the Lord's work.

In the UK Christians may feel vaguely uncomfortable about that, but any Christian entrusted with sizeable financial resources should be considering at least every legitimate way of being a faithful and profitable steward. The average church member would need expert professional help on such matters, but there are many organizations set up precisely to give advice to those willing to look for it.

For examples of organizations set up precisely to provide such professional advice, see the section on Financial Services in the *UK Christian Handbook*. (If your church has not yet got a copy, do recommend that it gets one – it may be somewhat pricey but it will prove a highly useful tool for all Christian organizations. Otherwise you should be able to consult a copy in your local reference library.)

World economic crises are daily in the news: OPEC nations at a conference table in the Middle East affect our petrol prices. High consumer nations import cheap products from economically impoverished countries while sending back manufactured goods that cost more and more; international companies buy land to produce export crops forcing local people to pay higher prices for their imported food. Producers dump grain in the ocean or pile butter into mountains just to keep prices high.

On a scale far greater than we can comprehend, many Christians ignorantly or glibly contribute to the economic injustice of the world, by shrugging off responsibility with a simple: 'But what can one person do?' God's response is in the singular: 'If anyone has material possessions and sees his brother in need but has no pity on him, how can the love of God be in him?' (1 John 3:17). Or, for even stronger words from the Lord, read Proverbs 24:11–12!

In all the areas we have considered, the influence of one person is small. But it is one by one that we shall stand before Him and give an account of our actions: 'wood, hay, straw,' or 'gold, silver and costly stones' (1 Corinthians 3:12–13). We are to be 'trustworthy in handling worldly wealth' so that the Lord might 'trust (us) with true riches' (Luke 16:11).

A Case Study in Financial Support

The team of senders we have been following are able to rejoice in this area of support:

> Because Lou and Sandy were our church's missionaries, we felt that there was a minimum amount of monthly support that needed to be raised by us before we went outside our fellowship for financial support. Early on, Lou had challenged all potential core group members to support this mission financially as concrete evidence of ownership.
>
> Financial support as well as prayer, moral and communication support was raised in this way: first our fellowship was made aware of Lou and Sandy's vision. One Sunday, Lou presented a slide show of a trip he and Sandy had taken to the Philippines several months before to see firsthand several ministry opportunities offered to them.
>
> For the next three Sundays after his presentation, the fellowship inserted into the church notice-sheet a commitment form with several boxes to tick including:

1) a commitment to support them financially with a space for how much and whether it was a one-off gift or monthly;
2) a commitment to support them in prayer;
3) a commitment to support them with letters.

We had a poster made with the 'Good Ship L, S and M' at one side. It was moveable and acted as the financial thermometer. The 'ship' moved weekly toward its destination as commitment forms came in for Lou, Sandy and Marlies.

Once the minimum amount of support was raised (an amount determined by the society they would be working with), Lou and Sandy then went to family and friends outside our fellowship for financial support.

After all support was committed, support packs were assembled and sent to each contributor. The packet contained:

1) A photo magnet of their family to put on the refrigerator.
2) A 'Coupon Book' with a two-year supply (this was the length of their commitment) of coupons which included the month and a space for the amount of support.
3) Twenty-four envelopes with our church's mailing address already affixed for easy mailing.

So far almost everyone has been great about keeping up with their monthly support. Each month our church sends a cheque to the organization's home office. From there the money is telexed to Lou and Sandy. We've been very blessed! Our fellowship has been so willing to support financially that we haven't had to come up with any unusual or emergency means to raise money for them. Praise the Lord!

What a blessing it is when people give so that His Good News can go forth. But there is more to the full measure of support needed by your cross-cultural worker. The nickname given to James (the brother of our Lord) was 'camel-knees' from all the time he spent in prayer. Consider the concert of *prayer* support you can offer to God on behalf of your worker.

(In addition to the individual study below, see the **Group Leader's Guide** for session four beginning on page 198.)

For Your Personal Involvement

- Paul had quite a bit to say about his financial support (or lack thereof)! Read each of the following passages and try to determine Paul's philosophy regarding financial support: 1 Corinthians 9; 2 Corinthians 12:13–19; Philippians 4:10–19; Philemon 18–22.
- Do an Old and New Testament word study on tithing. Discover that it is a principle of God's kingdom that works! Include Abraham's refusal to receive money from the King of Sodom, yet he himself gave a tithe to Melchizedek, King of Salem (Genesis 14; Hebrews 7:1–2).
- Without changing your spending patterns, keep a detailed record of your expenditure over one month. Then prayerfully begin listing areas in your lifestyle where there might possibly be unnecessary expense.
- Name several commercial jingles that, if followed, could easily distract you from giving financial support. What are you going to do to combat the impact of materialism in your life?

Action Steps

By the time you have read Chapter Four, completed the 'For Your Personal Involvement' section and participated in a group discussion, you should:

- Decide to purchase Doris Longacre's book *Living More With Less*. Read and apply it!
- Prepare a will.
- Know if you are to be a part of a missionary's Financial Support Team. If yes, let him know of your commitment. Find out where and how to send your cheque. Let him know the amount the Lord has put on your heart.
- Involve others. Look for others who have their finances in order and wish to see their funds used for the Kingdom of God.

Useful Addresses

Wallington Missionary Auction
20 Dalmeny Road
Carshalton
Surrey
SM5 4PP
Tel: 0181 6478437

Wallington Missionary Mart is associated with the above but handles less valuable, saleable but not auctionable items at:

105 Stafford Road
Wallington
Surrey
Tel: 0181 6693495
Website: www.wallingtonmissionary.org.uk

Northwood Missionary Auctions
Freepost
Northwood
Middlesex
HA6 3BS
Website: www.nmauctions.org.uk

Charity Aid Foundation (CAF)
25 Kings Hill Avenue
Kings Hill
West Malling
Kent
ME19 4TA
Tel: 01732 520000
Fax: 01732 520001
Website: www.cafonline.org

Macedonian Evangelical Trust
6 Eastmead Close
Bickley
Bromley
Kent
BR1 2JG
Tel: 0181 4678339

Maxco Trust
62 The Drive
Rickmansworth
WD3 4EB
Tel: 01923 710862

United Kingdom Evangelical Trust
Latchett Hall
Latchett Road
South Woodford
London
E18 1DL
Tel: 0181 5590114

Sovereign Giving
32 Highfields Mead
East Hanningfield
Chelmsford
CM3 8XA
Tel: 01245 403197
Fax: 01245 403037
Website: www.sovereign.giving.org.uk

Others are listed in the *UK Christian Handbook*.

Chapter Five

Prayer Support

*'And pray in the Spirit on all occasions with
all kinds of prayers and requests.'*
Ephesians 6:18a

In 1923 a teenager, Helen Mollenkof, attended a Keswick Conference in New Jersey. The speaker was L.L. Legters, who many years later with Cameron Townsend was to found Wycliffe Bible Translators.

God had given Legters a deep burden for all the indigenous people of Mexico and Central America without the Bible in their language. Speaking at the Keswick Conference, he challenged the young people to take the name of one language group in Mexico and pray for that people – that God would open doors so that His Word could be translated into the language of their hearts.

Helen Mollenkof was one of those who answered the challenge. She stepped forward and picked the name of a people she'd never heard of before: the Mazahua. She wrote the name on the flyleaf of her Bible. Then, closing her eyes, this teenage girl promised the Lord she would pray for them until they had the Bible translated into their own language.

Helen went ahead with life. She graduated from college, became a nurse and joined the Women's Union Missionary Society. Then she was sent to India, where she served as a missionary for the next thirty-five years. One of her ongoing prayer concerns was for the Mazahua people.

In 1967 Helen returned to the States to retire in Lancaster, Pennsylvania. Some time later, for some unexplained reason, she felt free to stop praying for the Mazahua people.

Then in 1981 she picked up her local newspaper and read an interview with Pat Hamric who, like herself, was a long-term missionary. As she read she discovered to her amazement that Pat, with Hazel Spotts and Don and Shirley Stewart, had been Bible translators among the Mazahua people.

Overjoyed, she found Pat's address and wrote to her: 'I thought you might be interested in my contact with the Mazahua Indians through prayer.'

She told Pat about the Keswick meeting, how L.L. Letgers had challenged them to take the name of one language group in Mexico, and her commitment to pray.

Pat replied, 'The New Testament is complete. It was dedicated in January 1970!'

Helen realized that January 1970 was the very time the Lord lifted her burden to pray!

Most of us are aware of the significance of prayer in God's global plan. We have powerful articles and books on the topic: *An Army of Intercessors: A Concert of Prayer; Seven Minutes with God; Mountain Movers; Praying the Four Ways Christ Taught; Power in Prayer; Destined for the Throne; Effective Prayer Life; Touch the World through Prayer; With Christ in the School of Prayer.*

What is the sum of their message? In the words of Augustine, 'Without God, we cannot; but without us, God will not.'

In His sovereignty, God has voluntarily linked Himself to human co-operation. He has inextricably bound Himself to the prayer of faith of His children. He merges His working with man's praying.

Though this is a deep mystery, it is clearly revealed in the Word and throughout history. Joshua's day in battle would have gone poorly without Moses' prayer (Exodus 17). Jacob's place in Israel's history would not have been the same without Penuel (Genesis 32). The cross would have been intolerable without Gethsemane (Luke 22).

Today one can stand in the room where John Wesley and the members of the 'Holy Club' held their prayer meetings, a force God used to ignite a revival that was felt around the world.

Consider Evan Roberts and his friends prostrating themselves before the Lord night after night, resulting in the Welsh Revival. The Prayer Mountain in Seoul, Korea, gave impetus to the growth of several of the largest churches in the world. The revival that swept Brazil meant that extra police were put on duty to control traffic in several major cities on prayer meeting night!

Prayer initiatives of each succeeding generation point to the vitality of intercession. In no greater arena of human activity is this mysterious union of our prayer and God's work seen than in the mission of the Church.

Jesus was going about all the cities and villages, teaching in their synagogues and preaching the gospel of the Kingdom, but when He saw the multitudes, He was moved with compassion. Then He said to His disciples, 'The harvest is plentiful but the workers are few. Ask the Lord of the harvest, therefore, to send out workers into his harvest field.' Three verses later, He sent them out two by two (Matthew 9–10)!

At the end of time, Christ the Lamb will be extolled: 'you were slain, and with your blood you purchased men for God from every tribe and language and people and nation' (Revelation 5:9). The twenty-four elders singing this new song will be holding golden vials full of incense that are the *prayers* of saints!

Paul in his masterful Ephesians 6 discourse on spiritual warfare not only clearly delineates the armour for our protection in war, but also identifies two of the major weapons of our warfare: the sword of the Spirit and prayer.

As a missionary of the first century, he was continually calling on the churches for prayer support: 'Brothers pray for us' he simply stated in 1 and 2 Thessalonians and Hebrews. His appeal to the Christians in Rome seemed a bit more pressing: 'I urge you brothers ... to join me in my struggle by praying to God for me' (Romans 15:30). Paul assumed Philemon was on his prayer support team (Philemon 22). To the church in Philippi, he stated his confidence that what he was experiencing would turn out well because of their prayers and the resources of the Spirit of Jesus Christ (Philippians 1:19) – bringing us back to that insoluble co-operation of God and man in prayer.

In spite of all of her lamentable weaknesses, appalling failures and indefensible shortcomings, the Church is the mightiest – the only – force contesting Satan's rule in human affairs! And that Church on her knees is the purifying and preserving influence which has kept the fabric of all we call civilization from total disintegration, decay and despair.

Samuel Chadwick said, 'The one concern of the devil is to keep Christians from praying. He fears nothing from prayerless studies, prayerless work and prayerless religion. He laughs at our toil, mocks at our wisdom, but trembles when we pray!'

Prayer is not begging God to do something He is loath to do. It is not overcoming God's reluctance to act. It is, rather, enforcing Christ's victory over Satan. It is the effective, fervent communication with the creator of the universe – in line with His will – which controls the balance of power in world affairs.

Prayer transcends the dimensions of time and space and ushers us into the very throne room of God, worshipping, petitioning and interceding in that spiritual realm of the eternal now.

Prayer is sometimes *alleluia* (Psalm 150). It is sometimes telling God the details of our needs (Philippians 4:6). It is sometimes labouring in unutterable groans of *intercession* (Romans 8:26). It is the prayer of a sending church that releases power through His messengers in China, Africa, Europe and Latin and North America.

Prayer is the arena of spiritual warfare. Those who enter there are in touch with a world in need. Those who enter there regularly know the scars but also the victory of battle.

Prayer is where the action is – supporting and sustaining those working overseas. It is vitally important for your cross-cultural worker to have a strong prayer support team every step of the way: from his calling to his building and training his whole support team – all before he even arrives abroad.

All Christians are involved in spiritual warfare. Wherever they are aggressively battling against the enemy, there is a greater vulnerability to his attacks. However, your cross-cultural worker often has to deal with battle tactics less familiar than those he faced at home. Where there is less Christian witness, there is greater oppression. Cultures more open to Eastern religions and animism are also more aware of the evil spirit world. Territory that

Satan has held for generations does not yield easily. Add to this your worker's adjusting to all the unknowns of their new culture, and you already have a sizeable prayer list.

However, because you may never have 'been there', his prayer needs may seem so remote, so unreal. Thus, you may sense a lack of being able to make your prayer specific for him.

Here is a prayer list to give you a good start in understanding the areas of need peculiar to a cross-cultural worker that make him vulnerable to discouragement. When you communicate with him, ask which of these areas are vital to him. And as you let him know of your commitment to sustain him in prayer, he will be happy to keep you informed of the more specific requests – especially if you ask in later communication how they were answered.

- Adjusting to the new language, different foods, new customs, hard climate.
- Protection in travel, health, accidents, dangerous situations.
- Parents' concern for their children's health, schooling, friendships. Housing accommodation, lack of privacy, differences in living standards, lack of accustomed conveniences.
- Loneliness, homesickness, lack of accustomed fellowship with others.
- Interpersonal relationships, dealing with their own (and others') prejudice, selfishness, depending on the faithfulness of others to meet financial needs.
- Effectiveness in ministry, whatever the assignment.
- Functioning of the tools of ministry. (It is amazing how printing presses break down just when a completed New Testament is ready for printing!)

- Lack of visible results; the 'ploughing, planting and watering' stages can go on for years!
- The people being ministered to, the national Christians, the leaders of the country.
- Need for stability, wisdom, compassion, self-discipline, boldness, power, love, to be filled with the Spirit of God.

A Model Prayer

Jo Shetler had completed the translation of the Balangao New Testament. A flourishing church had been established. She was now called back to the Philippines to be a speaker at the Balangao Bible Conference. Her subject was prayer.

She said that her prayer life had consisted of ' . . . all we ask God to do, such as heal our sicknesses, provide money to put children through school, give the ability to learn a language, translate Scripture and interact well with people.

'Then I decided to pray the prayers of Paul, David, and others in the Bible. I copied them out and started. What a surprise! Those people weren't asking God for the same things as I was! These 'model prayers' from Scripture seemed to centre more directly on God and his programme, rather than on people and their plans.'

Read all the articles on prayer; read all the books about prayer. But when you have finished, study and pray the prayers of the Bible!

One of the prayers of Paul fits perfectly the needs of the cross-cultural worker. He was praying it for the Christians in Colosse, but note how adaptable it is to the needs of any missionary.

Even before he prays, Paul twice assures those at Colosse that he is constantly praying for them. Look at Colossians 1:3,9: 'For this reason, since the day we heard about you, we have not stopped praying for you.'

Everyone who is interested in your missionary will at one time or another say a prayer for him. Certainly the Financial Support Team will pray as they write out their cheques, 'Lord, may they use this money wisely', or 'Lord, do they really need this money more than I do?'

The Communication Support Team will no doubt pray that the letters they put so much time into will arrive safely and minister to their missionary.

The Moral Support Team will surely whisper a prayer as they see their missionary's picture on the church notice board or when the pastor leads the congregation in a prayer for him.

But if you are going to be a part of your missionary's Prayer Support Team, your commitment must be more on the level of Paul's statement: 'For this reason, since the day we heard about you, we have not stopped praying for you.'

Here, then, is a 'model prayer' that you can pray for your cross-cultural worker, filling in the details with his specific personality and ministry needs:

'Asking God to fill you with the knowledge of His will . . .' (Colossians 1:9).

Once a worker arrives on the field, he is bombarded with an overwhelming array of ministry opportunities. Even if a predetermined job description has been established, there is always one more assignment to fit into the schedule. Joining a team short-handed through illness, furlough, or lack of labourers for an expanding ministry, every cross-cultural worker is faced with appeals to take on 'just a little bit more.'

Out of that mass of good deeds, your worker must discern those that were 'prepared in advance for [us] to do' (Ephesians 2:10).

Once he has heard God's will, a corollary prayer is for him to share judiciously with his supervisor that, in order to maintain his sanity, he must say 'no' to certain opportunities.

'through all spiritual wisdom and understanding . . .' (Colossians 1:9).

It is noteworthy that throughout Scripture these two qualities of the Christian life are always twins – one with the other. Wisdom can be defined as 'the ability to see things from God's perspective' and understanding as 'the facility to make that godly perspective work out in the affairs of this world.'

One missionary representative wisely said, 'The only people who know everything about missions are those who have been on the field less than six months!' Bombarded with cultural distinctives, worlds apart from his own culture, and quite possibly faced with methods that have become rutted in tradition, your worker continually needs to see things from God's perspective – things pertaining to his family life, his ministry, his relationship with nationals, his economy of time and energy, his finances, his prayer life, his relationships with ministers on his team and those of other groups.

It is not for nothing that Solomon urges: 'Get wisdom. Though it cost all you have, get understanding' (Proverbs 4:7).

As your prayers bind 'the strong man' (Matthew 12:29) so your worker can have a clear vision of eternal values from God's vantage point as your prayers elevate your missionary to be 'seated with [Christ] in the heavenly realms' (Ephesians 2:6). He must now understand how to make all that happen in the day-to-day affairs of his life.

Days – even weeks – of extended travel away from home wreak havoc with scheduled family time. Dare we use God's money to take a holiday? How do I tell the nationals that we aren't going to use foreign money for their building – that it is better for the congregation to trust God for the provision? How do I not violate my doctrinal distinctives, yet develop a working relationship with others in the body of Christ? These and a thousand questions bombard your worker's life and demand an understanding heart (see 1 Kings 3:9). To see things from God's perspective is one thing (wisdom); to know how to make them work out in your missionary's day-to-day life is another (understanding).

You can see how this prayer for wisdom and understanding could consume hours of intercession as you wage war against the enemy.

'That you may live a life worthy of the Lord and may please him in every way' (Colossians 1:10).

Phillips' translation puts it, 'That your outward lives which men see may bring credit to your Master's Name.' Watchman Nee said, 'If you want to be a missionary to China, plan on wearing a "learner's permit" around your neck for the first ten years!' Because of diverse cultural distinctives and your cross-cultural worker's lack of ability to communicate deeply, it is often only the love of Christ working out through his life that tells the gospel message.

Another perspective of this, of course, is that 'What you are doing speaks so loudly, I can't hear what you are saying!' When your worker's actions differ from his words, it will be his actions that the people among whom he ministers will believe.

The enemies of the cross gave the name 'Christian' (little Christ) to the believers in Antioch (see Acts 11:26). It was a dirty word then, but since the followers of The Way were living epistles, known and read by all men, they were easily identifiable. Are we so easy to identify?

A team of college students walked into a remote village in Central America where there were no Christians. Their job was to paint a school building a previous team had built. Because they were excited to share the Lord, the weight of their luggage, paint and equipment seemed light.

As they entered the square, they were met by the village chief. He told them his people had heard all they needed to about this man Jesus. 'We don't want to hear another word you might have to say. Just paint our school building as you said you would. We will watch you. When you have finished, we will let you know if we want your Jesus.'

The team knew their outward lives would be living letters 'from Christ, written . . . on tablets of human hearts' (2 Corinthians 3:2–3). All they believed about the Word was put to the test in that village.

Those students 'lived a life worthy of the Lord'; when they were ready to leave, ten people including the village Chief trusted in Christ as their Saviour!

'. . . bearing fruit in every good work' (Colossians 1:10).

There are two considerations for prayer here:

1) That your missionary will be involved in 'good work'. Unfortunately, there may be thousands of hours of effort that aren't even aimed at decisive points of battle.

Your prayers will release the Spirit's guidance in developing a specific strategy 'in every good work' for your missionary. Your prayers of intercession will open his eyes to decisive points of battle.

2) Thus, being involved in good works, you and your worker are interested in seeing 'fruit that will last.' To give birth to a child is (to say the least) hard work! Yet, the Bible says 'A woman . . . when her baby is born . . . forgets the anguish because of her joy' (John 16:21). To raise a child in godliness is incomparably more difficult.

To be used of the Spirit to give birth to a child spiritually and cross-culturally is hard work! To nurture that child to maturity demands the patient endurance of years.

It is true that one sows, another waters, but the Lord gives the increase (see 1 Corinthians 3:6).

'. . . growing in the knowledge of God' (Colossians 1:10).

The personal devotional life of your worker is at stake here. Overseas there are many factors that can lead to spiritual drought:

1) Your worker may become so busy 'working for the Lord' that there is no time for personal intake. His head can still nod at the appropriate times; his public prayers can still sound almost angelic; his teaching can still be most proper! But the life of the Spirit is gone.
2) Loneliness haunts many cross-cultural workers. More susceptible, of course, are single adults. This can lead to seeking inappropriate relationships, which can lead to spiritual drought.

3) Failure takes its toll on some. High Western expecta-
   tions are not met. Discouragement debilitates. This
   downward spiral of morale is as slippery as grease. At
   the bottom of the slide are many spiritually depleted
   field workers. Often these burned-out workers do not
   realize they should go home. They become an
   embarrassment to the mission endeavour, a drain on
   the energies of others who are trying to help them and
   a dismal blot on the testimony of God's Church in the
   world!
4) Disillusionment can bring awful frustration, which in
   turn may lead to spiritual drought. In the mission
   process there are many tasks that aren't very
   glamorous – cleaning the grease trap outside the
   kitchen door, keeping an inventory of radio parts, or
   being reviled by a drunken street-sleeper.
5) Your worker may become discontented with other
   workers. 'Discontent' is putting it mildly! 'Radical
   interpersonal relationship problems' might be more
   accurate. This is the number one cause of missionary
   failure. Why? Because Jesus said, 'They [the ones your
   worker has gone out to seek and to save] will know
   you are my disciples if you love one another' (John
   13:35). So here is a major area of attack by the enemy:
   if he can destroy our unity he will destroy our
   testimony!

Your prayers and the united intercession of the Prayer
Support Team for your cross-cultural worker will put a
hedge of protection around him (Ezekiel 22:30), will
guard his thoughts (Philippians 4:4–7) and will give him
the wisdom of a peacemaker in those tough interpersonal
situations (James 3:13–18).

'. . . strengthened with all power according to his glorious might' (Colossians 1:11).

In Acts 1:4 and 8 Jesus gave clear instructions to His disciples to wait for the power of the Holy Spirit. It's a jungle out there! It is insane to step into cross-cultural outreach ministry without 'his glorious might.' It is imperative to have a vital, personal, alive, active, growing, dynamic, real relationship with the third person of the Godhead, the Holy Spirit.

Intercede for your cross-cultural worker that he would be continually being 'filled with the Spirit' (Ephesians 5:18). Pray that he will daily 'have [his mind] set on what the Spirit desires' (Romans 8). Life and ministry in a second culture (actually, we all walk in an alien world!) hold challenges foreign to your worker but not to the Spirit of God. As you pray, the Spirit of truth will guide him into all truth (John 16:13).

'that you may have great endurance and patience . . . joyfully' (Colossians 1:11).

Joe and Sue were ready to leave Brazil. Because they had stayed several months over the two-year visa issued, the federal government in Brasilia had provided them with a letter assuring them all was in order. However, when on departure they presented that letter and their passports (which showed an expired visa) to the state official, he looked at Joe and said, 'You are in our country illegally! That will be a $500 fine!' Not having the money, Joe and Sue spent three long days, returning to that official trying to convince him (through an interpreter) to let them go. Finally, finding a way to let him 'save face', he came up with an idea and stamped their exit visa.

Missionaries, particularly those in Two-Thirds World ministries, are more than familiar with bank queues, petrol queues, food queues and delays in mail deliveries, material deliveries and baby deliveries! Patience and longsuffering are critical.

But there is another word: 'joyfully'. Yes, your worker might in stoicism realize he has no alternative than to wait. But can he brush off the cobwebs of delay joyfully? Can the joy of the Lord be his strength as after a two-hour wait in line he steps up to the bank clerk's window to be told, 'Sorry, we are going on strike right now!'?

Yes, your prayers like sweet incense intercede for him before the Father day and night, meting out to him the measure of grace sufficient for any trial. Prayer is where the action is.

'giving thanks to the Father' (Colossians 1:12).

Paul enjoined the Christians in Philippi, 'Do not be anxious about anything, but in everything, by prayer and petition, with thanksgiving, present your requests to God' (Philippians 4:6). A thankful attitude reveals a heart that is right with God.

The pressures of the mission field, however, can produce in your worker something other than a thankful attitude. The difficult living conditions can say, 'It's not fair!' The depleting of finances each month can shout, 'I need more!' The lack of apparent spiritual response can cry, 'You're not worth my time!' The breakdown in health can cause us to think, 'I guess God didn't really call me to these people!'

Your prayers can be used to challenge your missionary with Mordecai's words: 'Who knows but that you have come to royal position for such a time as this?' (Esther 4:14). Your prayers can be used to help your cross-cultural worker identify with Paul: 'I consider that our present sufferings are not worth comparing with the glory that will be revealed in us' (Romans 8:18). Your prayers can be used to stir the resources that will build in your field worker an attitude of thankfulness: 'It is a privilege to be about my Father's business.'

In-the-Gap Praying

'I looked for a man among them who would build up the wall and stand before me in the gap on behalf of the land, so that I would not have to destroy it, but I found none' (Ezekiel 22:30).

The 'gap' mentioned in Ezekiel has been used to express a number of concepts. Prophetically Jesus came to bridge the chasm between God and man. As an appeal to people to go to the mission fields of the world, filling in the 'gap' of front-line workers is critical. There are cultural gaps between the missionary and the people group he is trying to reach.

But in the context of Ezekiel, 'in the gap' speaks more directly of the role of an intercessor – one who forms a barrier (a wall) between God (who is speaking) and 'the land, so that I would not have to destroy it.'

'I looked for a man . . .' Abraham became that man: 'God, will you not spare the city for fifty righteous men? Forty-five? Forty? Thirty? Twenty? Ten? Far be it from you to kill the righteous with the wicked . . . Will not the Judge of all the earth do right?' (See Genesis 18.) Those are powerful words for one who had 'been so bold as to speak to the Lord, though [he was] but dust and ashes!' He stood in the gap.

'I looked for a man . . .' Moses became that man: 'But Moses sought the favour of the Lord his God. "O Lord," he said, "why should your anger burn against your people?"' Just four verses earlier, in His anger God had called them Moses' people! After two more verses of intercession, 'the Lord relented and did not bring on his people the disaster he had threatened' (Exodus 32:11–14).

Another time Moses more boldly said: 'But now, please forgive their sin – but if not, then blot me out of the book you have written' (Exodus 32:32). Read Deuteronomy 9 for a review of the many times Moses stood in the gap for his people. Moses was definitely an 'in-the-gap' intercessor!

'I looked for a man...' Aaron became that man (Numbers 16). Nehemiah became that man (Nehemiah). Jesus became that man (John 17). Paul became that man (Romans 9). Others through the generations have become men and women who stood in the gap.

And today Scripture still declares the voice of God – which perhaps says to you, 'I looked for you to build the wall, to stand in the gap!'

A battle is raging for the souls of men and women. In the book of Job, we have been given some insight into the spiritual realm from which this war emanates.

Job had arrived! He was rich. He was famous. He was perfect and upright. He feared God and hated evil. At least this is what the world could see.

But behind the scenes of this visible world is the real world. And Satan saw the hedge complete – not only around Job, but 'around his household and everything he has' (Job 1:1–10). Two excellent novels, *This Present Darkness* and *Piercing the Darkness* by Frank Peretti, give thought-provoking possibilities to the subtleties of this behind-the-scenes war (see Resources, pages 209–20).

The 'accuser of our brothers' (Revelation 12:10) is 'going to and fro' in the earth, and, 'prowls around looking for someone to devour' (1 Peter 5:8). When he sees the breach in the hedge, the broken-down walls, the secret thoughts of sin, his entrance to the minds and hearts of men is with ease.

And even when that hedge is complete around a man, Satan presents himself before God. It's those 'perfect ones' he wants to get. So God, knowing his thoughts, says, 'Have you considered my servant Job?' (Job 1:8).

This is one of the works of the enemy: to set his heart on even the elect, if it were possible (see Matthew 24:24). Jesus said, 'Simon, Satan has asked to sift you as wheat, but I have prayed for you' (Luke 22:31,32). Satan and a third of the host of heaven who rebelled against God with him are out to destroy to whatever degree and with whatever diabolical consequences they can contrive.

Picture the scene in that heavenly throne room, that secret place you enter boldly to obtain mercy and grace to help in the time of need (Hebrews 4:16). Not only are you and God there as you intercede for the 'mercy and grace' your cross-cultural worker needs, but also present is the adversary. The enemy of our souls is telling the truth about our weaknesses or lying through his teeth about us, using any tactic in his fiendish reservoir to break through the hedge, to rush through the gap.

One of the strongest weapons to bind the work of the enemy is the intercessory, effectual, fervent prayer of a committed, united team of believers.

The Prayer Support Team should never be limited in number. A missionary relates: 'One morning while trying to watch my son's surgery, I "decided" to faint! In the process, I sustained a fractured skull and serious concussion. For three weeks I lay flat in bed and lived from one painkiller to the next. All the missionaries in the area were praying. But one night my wife got on the radio to solicit additional prayer from the team back home. She contacted our pastor's wife just as she was preparing to go to a church prayer meeting. Following that burst of intercession, I never took another painkiller. I had no more pain. To God be the glory!'

Unbelief is the single most serious factor that breaks down the wall. God is looking for a team, for a woman, for a man who will 'build up the wall and stand before me in the gap on behalf of the land so that I would not have to destroy it, but I found none!' And, in the Ezekiel account, destruction came!

May it not be said of us on that awesome judgement day that He was calling from among us a man, a woman, a Prayer Support Team to stand in the gap, but He found none!

Rather may it be said, 'Well done, good and faithful servant! . . . Come and share your master's happiness!' (Matthew 25:21.)

Fasting and Prayer

In a trilogy of instructions in what has become known as the Sermon on the Mount, Jesus said, 'When you give . . . when you pray . . . when you fast.' He presumes that we will fast. He follows each injunction with contrasting instruction: 'Don't do it this way; but do do it this way' (Matthew 6:1–18).

Unfortunately, today what most Christians know about fasting and food is fast food!

The biblical significance of fasting, however, is so profound throughout the Old and New Testaments that for us to be ignorant of or indifferent toward its place in a Christian's life is equal to spiritual starvation.

'But I'll starve to death!' is exactly the way many Christians respond. Therefore, we need to know the 'what, why, when, and how' of fasting.

What is fasting? Both in the secular sense and in the biblical sense, fasting means abstaining from food. A total fast is abstaining from all food and drink (Exodus 34:28). A normal fast allows the intake of drink (Luke 4:2). A limited fast indicates restriction of certain types of foods (Daniel 10:2–3). Prayer and care must be taken in choosing the type of fast to enter.

Why should we fast? Because Jesus told us to. Isaiah gave clear spiritual and physical reasons for the exercise of fasting:

a) Spiritual: 'To loose the chains of injustice and untie the cords of the yoke, to set the oppressed free, and break every yoke.'
b) Physical: 'To share your food with the hungry, and to provide the poor wanderer with shelter – when you see the naked, to clothe him, and not to turn away from your own flesh and blood' (Isaiah 58:6–7).

When should we fast? Definitely not when Christ the bridegroom is around: 'But when the bridegroom will be taken from them, then they will fast' (Matthew 9:14–15). As we still await the return of the bridegroom, now is the time for fasting!

How should we fast? Definitely 'do not look sombre as the hypocrites do for they disfigure their faces to show men they are fasting . . . But . . . put oil on your head and wash your face so that it will not be obvious, . . . and your Father who sees in secret will reward you' (Matthew 6:17,18).

Because our bodies are meant to take in food, and there is no spiritual merit in injuring our bodies through fasting, there are other important 'do's and don'ts' we must consider as we enter and conclude a time of fasting. The finest work on the subject of fasting is Arthur Wallis' *God's Chosen Fast* (see Resources, page 212).

When prayer and fasting are practised together, they present a unique and powerful duo. Incorporate the practice of fasting with your prayer support.

Prayer for More Field Workers

Jesus left His outreach headquarters, Capernaum. 'He went about all the cities and villages, teaching in their synagogues and preaching the gospel of the Kingdom, healing every sickness and disease among the people.'

A gruelling itinerary. A heavy schedule. But on one occasion, 'when he saw the crowds, he had compassion on them because they were harassed and helpless, like sheep without a shepherd.

'Then he turned to his disciples, "The harvest is plentiful but the workers are few. Ask the Lord of the harvest, therefore, to send out workers into his harvest field."' (Matthew 9:35–8.)

Having painted a picture of a vast harvest, Jesus shared His means for reaping the harvest: field workers! His harvesters are ordinary human beings who will be obedient to His Great Commission – people who know Him sharing with people who don't.

Jesus tells us to pray to the Father that He will send them forth. There is a crying need for field workers today; this is still a most needed prayer. But be careful when you pray it. Remember that several verses later He sent forth the very men He had instructed to pray!

Prayer for an Entrance of the Gospel

Paul solicited the prayers of the Christians in Colosse with these words: 'And pray for us too, that God may open a door for our message, so that we may proclaim the mystery of Christ' (Colossians 4:3).

Our prayers should be that the gospel – the mystery of Christ – no longer remains a mystery to them, but enters through the door of their hearts.

Often a 'door' that will open into a culture is a story or tradition in that culture which encourages a receptivity to the gospel. In missiological circles these are called 'redemptive analogies.'

For example, missionary Bruce Olson found that the Motilone Indians of the jungles of Colombia had a ceremony in which they cried for a god to come out of a hole dug in the ground. Olson used this tradition as a bridge to tell the Motilone of the resurrected Christ – who came out of his tomb, a 'hole in the ground'!

Three of the best books on this subject are, *Eternity in Their Hearts* and *Peace Child* by Don Richardson, and *The Discovery of Genesis* by C.H. Kang and Ethel R. Nelson (see Resources, pages 209–220).

So pray for opening doors as your field workers try to discover redemptive analogies for the people among whom they work.

Prayer to Bind the Strong Man

As Paul told the Christians in Corinth that he would stay in Ephesus until Pentecost, he said, 'because a great door for effective work has opened to me, and there are many who oppose me' (1 Corinthians 16:9).

Behind every open door of opportunity, there are enemies of the cross – always one with a foot stuck out to trip up those who would walk through. Sometimes the enemy is even able to use the actions of other believers to thwart plans!

There is a time to resist the devil (James 4:7). There is a time to cast out devils (Mark 16:17). There is a time to bind the works of the enemy, to bind the 'strong man' himself (Matthew 18:18; Mark 3:27). And there is a time to inhibit his activity and pseudo-authority in the affairs of men (1 John 3:8).

This takes bold men and women praying bold prayers, for the enemy does not like being exposed for the fraud he is.

Prayer for His Kingdom to Come

Jesus said it so simply: 'When you pray, say ... "your kingdom come"' (Luke 11:2). Pray for the people into whose lives the Kingdom has not yet come.

More than three billion individuals in thousands of distinct people groups are today without a solid gospel witness, many with no knowledge of even the name of Jesus Christ. Thousands of souls die every day without a chance to respond to the message of salvation in Christ.

And we are not talking only about those who live in deep, dark jungles. An evangelist was sitting with his team at the breakfast table of a hotel restaurant in Singapore, a city/nation that enjoys a higher standard of living than the United States and is home to thousands of believers. The group had their Bibles out, and the waitress asked them what that book was. 'The Bible', they told her. Her response: 'What is a Bible?' She had never heard of such a book!

Pray for fallow ground to be broken up (Jeremiah 4:3). Pray for the seed to fall on fertile soil (Matthew 13:3–9). Pray that the waterers will neither drench nor parch the seedling. Pray that the cultivators will not mar the plant by misusing their tools. Pray that the Lord of the harvest will give the increase (1 Corinthians 3:6).

What a privilege that He allows us to participate in His plan of the ages by coming boldly before Him, interceding on behalf of the lost of the world as well as for the workers who have gone out to the fields of the world. If God be for us, who can be against us? What an unequal contest it seems!

It is prayer that links the missionary enterprise to the irresistible power of God. Prayer is the decisive point on which the battle turns. The mightiest weapon we can use is the weapon of prayer – potent, powerful, prevailing prayer, the prayer of faith against which the adversary has no effective counterweapon. 'Pray without ceasing' (1 Thessalonians 5:17).

Case Study in Prayer Support

How does the core group we have been following handle prayer support?

Our prayer support for Lou and Sandy is much harder to talk about than the other areas of support. For example, as regards financial support, we can discuss how we raised monthly support and then have the concrete evidence every month, when the cheques come in, that people are following through their commitment.

But prayer support is a little more difficult. At best we can say how we've tried to encourage people to pray, and how we pray that they are following through their commitment.

One element of prayer support is an awareness of needs. Lou and Sandy's needs are made known in several ways:

1) Everyone committed to support them in prayer is encouraged to have one clock in their house set to Filipino time (16 hours ahead). When we wake up at 6 a.m. and realize that it is 10 p.m. the next day in the Philippines, it can prompt us to pray with an increased awareness – perhaps for a good night's sleep!

2) Lou and Sandy have a monthly newsletter they send out to supporters with a specific section summarizing their prayer needs. This portion of the letter can be cut out, highlighted and stuck to the refrigerator with the photo magnet of Lou and Sandy that each supporter received in their initial packet.

3) Two prayer chains have been formed. A prayer chain is simply a list of names and phone numbers. As a prayer request is made known via letter, phone call or email, the person at the top of the list is notified. He phones the next person on the list who then relays the message to the next person and so on until all are made aware of the need.

Two prayer chains were developed for this reason: it was felt that there could be times when a need would arise of such a personal nature that it might be best if only the core group and a few others determined by Lou and Sandy knew about it in detail. The second prayer chain would receive that prayer request in more general terms. Other requests may be given to both groups.

Another element of prayer support is to be able to intercede as led by the Holy Spirit without even knowing the needs. Or, perhaps, the information we receive about their needs doesn't indicate the real need at all! It is necessary for us then, by the Spirit, to perceive the real needs as we get together in intercession for Lou and Sandy and the people among whom they're ministering. We're always trying to expand our prayer so we include the people group; Lou and Sandy will be coming home one day, and it seems only reasonable for us to develop hearts for the needs of those people now so that we can keep praying for God's activity among them for years to come.

One way in which we are attempting to increase the efficacy of our prayers was expressed in a recent mailing we sent out to all prayer supporters. In it we asked for volunteers to make a weekly commitment to fast and pray for one hour. We suggested a dinner fast (actually starting right after lunch) with a prayer time following in the evening. We also stated that if they felt led to commit themselves to a longer fast or even a partial fast, this was certainly between them and the Lord. We asked them to make it a four-month commitment and to complete an enclosed form detailing what day they had chosen to fast. This has been on a strictly voluntary basis. The results in terms of commitment will ultimately be seen in a new release of the Lord's power in Lou and Sandy as they go about their work.

There is so much to learn in this area of support. May the Lord grant us ever willing hearts to grow in prayer and may we be ever submissive to get down on our knees and be about our Father's business through prayer.

Prayer is truly a powerful weapon to be used in the spiritual conflicts encountered in cross-cultural ministry. Yet, again, there are other aspects of your worker's life that must be considered. He will also want you to keep in touch with him through *communication* support.

[In addition to the individual study below, see the **Group Leader's Guide** for session five beginning on page 199.]

For Your Personal Involvement

- Keep a record for one week of the prayers you pray. Is there a good mixture of praise, personal petition, intercession and thanksgiving?
- Study the prayers of several Bible characters. (Be sure to include the publican's prayer in Luke 18:13!) Or read through all the prayers of one person. Identify each as a prayer of thanksgiving, praise, personal petition or intercession. Become familiar with the way the prayer sounds. Compare (or contrast) them with your style of praying.
- Locate, read and study the nineteen recorded prayers of Jesus.
- Begin or become part of a missions prayer group where you can learn to participate in the power of united prayer.
- Read Arthur Wallis' book *God's Chosen Fast*.

Action Steps

By the time you have read Chapter Five, completed the 'For Your Personal Involvement' section and participated in a discussion group, you should:

- More closely pray the prayers of the Bible. Be on guard against the ever-popular 'gimme' prayers.
- Be able to decide if prayer support is a commitment you can make to your missionary. If you can, write to him, letting him know of that commitment and of your desire to be kept informed of his prayer needs.
- Practise the Christian discipline of fasting.
- Pray without ceasing!
- Involve others. Actively look for others in your circle of relationships who have, or who might develop, a heart for prayer.

Chapter Six

Communication Support

'I hope in the Lord Jesus to send Timothy to you soon,
that I also may be cheered when I receive news about you.'
Philippians 2:19

'I had no knowledge of missions and no preparation, whatsoever! I knew God wanted me to go to Paris, but even that was only confirmed in my heart after I arrived there. My home church's "policy" was to lay hands on you, say a prayer and wave, "Goodbye!" My home fellowship group said they would write to me and pray for me. I wrote to them faithfully about every five weeks. I received one letter from them the first year and one the second!

'Lack of communication further hit me when I arrived. I was to work with another missionary from my church who was helping equip lay leaders in a new church near the Latin Quarter. When I got there, I found out that he had moved to another city!

'A local national church took me in. I began learning servanthood in a cross-cultural setting. Sweeping, cleaning toilets, dusting, sorting clothes and running errands were my first assignments. After I regained my ability in the language, I began teaching in their day school for children.

'Lack of communication also hit my wallet. I arrived in Paris with very little money and a promise of a temporary place to stay. (Remember, I had had no training.) I was never taught how to raise financial support. I had not communicated my needs before I left, nor in my letters once I had gone. I thought it was bad to talk about money. Now I know I should give full information and allow others to share in His ministry that way.

'I got a small cheque from a friend through my church the first month. Well into the second month I asked my brother to phone my church to see if any money had come in for me and if they had sent it. Only $45 had come in and that had been sent, returned for postage, and posted again! Anyway, I moved ten times that first year because I had to live wherever I could without paying rent.

'By then I had come to accept it: this is missionary life – until I met Bill and Louise. It began when they offered to help me financially. I felt bad because their church was supporting them and they were using some of it to help me. Yet, my church was doing nothing to help me.

'As I got to know them better, I saw that not only were their finances in order, but a whole communication network was in place. Regular mail. Frequent care parcels. Phone calls of friendship (not of desperation, like mine).

'But I really saw how it could be when their church's cross-cultural co-ordinator, John, came to visit them. It was just a one-day visit as he was in Europe on other business, but I saw real caring. He had prepared a special Bible study that he said the Lord had given him just for them. He brought a banner saying, "We really do miss you!" It had personal notes scribbled all over it. There were special goodies for their children.

'I came to realize that communication, prayer and financial support was strong from their sending church – to that extent their ministry was strong. John said I could call on them any time there was a need. He didn't know the extent of my hurting. (Or did he?) I received a letter once a year from my church telling me what they were doing (yes, I was even listed as one of their "accomplishments"!), but they never once asked me how I was doing! I had a lot of anger and hurt inside towards my church before coming back, because I felt they didn't care.

'After two years I did come home. And I realized the misunderstanding was as much a result of my failure to communicate as theirs. I was open with my home group. I learned that they thought the church was supporting me and I thought they knew of my condition and need! We just hadn't communicated!

'I got some good training in communication skills. I learned to be open in sharing my needs for communication as well as for prayer, finances and the other areas of support.

'I am back in Paris, now. No, I don't expect a visit from anyone from my church with banners and goodies. But I do have an established foundation of a strong and growing support team from my home group and other individuals in my church and family. And we're communicating! May God be praised!'

It is hard to imagine the importance of communication from home until you have 'been there.' When a person or family arrives overseas to establish their new routine, real loneliness can set in – a feeling of isolation, of being out of it. A new missionary can feel, 'They have forgotten me!' 'They aren't writing' might be interpreted: 'They don't care! I'm out of their sight – and therefore out of their mind! And I'm going out of mine!'

One family recently returned to Israel, this time with two children. The wife recalls, 'The first two weeks I was filled with guilt for doing this to my children. I had taken them away from the grandparents who cherish them and whom they adore. I had taken them away from *Sesame Street*, a wonderful library, swimming lessons and food they love. I had taken them away from carpeted floors, litter-free parks with grass instead of broken glass, cool weather, Sunday school – from friends, drinkable water that doesn't make them ill, a familiar doctor I can trust, a car instead of a bus or having to walk in the blazing sun and a mother with lots of energy, patience and joy!

'Well,' she says, 'a phone call from Amy back in my home town revealed that she had felt the same way when she first went to Greece. I still wasn't completely convinced that I was doing the best for my boys; but if Amy got through it – and her kids are great . . . and I do trust God who is my Father and theirs, who only wants the best for us . . .

'After the call, I began to think, "To tell the truth, David and Daniel seem to be adapting more quickly than I am!" Two-year-old David even reminded me of a Hebrew word that I couldn't think of the other day. And Daniel has learned how to fall on these hard floors without getting a big bump on his head.

The missionary concludes, 'Even my mother is handling this well. She recently encouraged me in a letter: "God wants you there, Mary. Your kids could be ill here, too. C'mon, toughen up!" It seems every time we get discouraged, some bit of communication comes through to encourage us!'

Communicating Through Letters

Though Paul, the most prolific New Testament writer, did not have access to the telephone or fax, a modern postal system, email or a computer chatroom, he knew the importance of personal communication. His letters are shot through with personal comments:

- Requests for his support team to 'bring his cloak' when they come to him and 'especially the parchments' (2 Timothy 4:13).
- An earnest appeal to 'prepare a guest room for me' (Philemon 22).
- In his powerful letter to the Christians in Rome – that great treatise on grace – he devotes almost all of chapter 16 to personal messages. No less than forty-one people are specifically mentioned. Tertius, who has been writing the Roman letter for Paul, might have got so excited about all this exchange of greetings that he leaned over and nudged Paul: 'Paul, may I say "Hi," too?' Verse 22 reads, 'I, Tertius, send my Christian greetings also!'

James personalized his short letter seventeen times by referring to the dispersed tribes as 'my brothers.' John, when writing to his friend Gaius and again to 'the elect lady,' found it difficult to put into words all he wanted to say (2 John 12; 3 John 13). Yet in writing his gospel he wanted a scroll the size of the whole world to write everything that was on his heart (John 21:25). Luke, for the sake of his friend Theophilus, 'carefully investigated everything from the beginning', to set in order the record of the gospel of Christ and the Acts of the Apostles (Luke 1:1–4).

Peter and Paul found it not 'burdensome' to remind their readers again and again of especially important things (2 Peter 1:12; Philippians 3:1). Jude, as he sat to write his brief letter, intended to make it a light, happy one, rejoicing in their common salvation. But as he took pen in hand, the Spirit of God compelled him to exhort them to 'contend for the faith' (Jude 3).

Whether on parchment or paper or through cyber-space, letter writing is the easiest, most common way of keeping in touch; it is the mainstay of communication.

What to Communicate

The content of your communication is vital. Say things that really matter. Not just, 'How are you? I am fine. Went shopping today. Had meat loaf for dinner.' (Of course, they'll read anything from home! But . . .)

Rather, share your thoughts and feelings – what is really going on in your life. How is God working in you? Be realistic and honest but don't use them as your coun-sellors. Remember, you are their support.

Get involved in their lives overseas as much as you can. Ask questions about their lives there and respond to what they have said in their previous letters to you. This is especially encouraging because it shows that you really read their letters and are interested enough for some follow-up conversation about it.

One sending team member says, 'My wife and I are on the Communication Support Team of over eighty missionaries. We receive forty to fifty letters every month. When I read their letters, I have a pen in hand to jot down notes or circle specific thoughts I want to respond to. This is the only way we can answer that many letters! And it will work for you, as well.'

Share how God is leading you to pray for them. Ask for their specific and personal prayer requests and updates on things about which you previously prayed.

Share a particularly meaningful sermon you have just heard, church news or news about a mutual friend – edifying news, of course!

When communicating with missionaries serving in restricted-access countries where their ministry may be considered illegal, be sure to check with your church or missionary society for guidelines when writing about Christian matters and ministries.

Don't forget to get your kids to write to the children in your missionary family. This is good training for them to become aware of and involved in missions! Also, grandmas and grandpas, aunts and uncles: keep in contact with your grandchildren, nieces and nephews. They need to hear from you.

Let's look back at the biblical writers referred to for some patterns for you to follow in your letters to your cross-cultural workers:

Paul to the Romans: Use names to make the stories real. Instead of, 'Everyone says "Hi!"' give the names of specific people they know who said "Hi."'

James to the dispersed tribes: Make it a friendly letter, and personalize it. Even though (or maybe, because) James had some tough things to say, he reminded them of the personal relationship uniting them. 'Though miles separate us, we are still friends; you are not forgotten' is the feeling communicated when you make the letter personal.

John to Gaius and the 'elect lady': The time will come when it is tough to sit down and write. You don't know what to say or how to say it. Probably the single greatest hindrance to letter writing is waiting for a big block of time. Don't wait – it will probably never come!

It is not so important to be organized or have nice paper or be able to write pages and pages. What is important is to do it! Jot down a thought or two on any piece of paper. A day or so later when you have another thought, write it down. When you have accumulated a 'letter's worth,' send it. Of course, it would help to number the pieces of paper!

A missionary recalls, 'One of my favourite letters came on John F. Kennedy Airport tissue paper, written while a support team friend was waiting for an international flight. The novelty of it assured me of the instant inspiration of the words written!'

John to readers of his Gospel: Don't feel that you have to write every word of every conversation of every friend of theirs for every day they are gone. Allow the Spirit to guide you to share incidents and stories that are uplifting, informative and motivating.

How you say things also has its impact. Consider the following contrast:
'Well, Jerry has taken your place and is doing such a great job with your home group that everything is just fine without you' and 'Wow! God's timing is so perfect. Just as He called you to Alma Ata, He raised up Jerry to continue the good work you were doing with the home group.'

Luke to Theophilus: Be accurate in your reporting to your friends. Distance and time and cultures already have their way of distorting facts. Memory blurs. You want to communicate a true report of what's going on among people at home.

Peter and Paul to readers of their Epistles: With Peter and Paul sometimes you will say, 'I do not tire of reminding you again and again to be diligent in your personal devotion to God.' Don't be afraid to encourage and exhort with the same themes and reminders often – as the Spirit directs you.

Jude to those called of God: As you get in to the habit of regular letter writing, you will begin anticipating what you want to say. As you listen to the words of a new song on the radio, you realize how they would minister to your friend. You jot them down. As you return to a familiar spot or a favourite restaurant, a pleasant memory inspires you to relate an incident. So you sit down to write, just wanting to rejoice about the good things of life. But don't be surprised if there is also a stirring in your soul as the Holy Spirit says, 'I have an important message for you to share. Warn him to be on his guard for "godless men who change the grace of our God . . ."' (Jude 4).

Other Ways of Communicating

This need for contact with 'home' is nothing new. You remember the story of David, away from his home in Bethlehem. In the heat of battle, he longed for a drink of water from his favourite well over by the city gate (2 Samuel 23:15). His son, Solomon, said, 'Like cold water to a weary soul, is good news from a distant land' (Proverbs 25:25). The need for news from home isn't new at all, but our world has certainly advanced in its methods of communication.

The telephone, for example, lets you call almost anywhere in the world at reasonable cost. You wouldn't use this method as regularly as a letter, but even just once can be really appreciated. You can be led by the Spirit to phone at a time in your missionary's life when he most needs it.

A communicating sender says, 'Once I was reading a letter from our cross-cultural worker. It wasn't so much what the letter said (since it had been written two weeks before) as the Spirit quickening my mind to understand her present need. I checked the time. It should be about 7 a.m. in Israel. She should still be at home. I dialled. On the second ring, I heard her voice. And we talked for a few minutes. What did we say? I can't remember! But she still talks about that phone call that came at just the right time!'

Faxed messages and telexes can communicate with cross-cultural workers who may only have access to this level of technology. The work of communicating is still there. But these devices make the exchange of ideas more rapid and convenient.

Ham radio is an exciting communicating channel. If your worker is in a more remote part of the world, he may know a ham radio operator. If so, ask him to give you the call letters and the times he is usually on the air. Then find an operator in your area. These people are usually happy to set up a 'phone patch' for you to talk with your friend – often free! Around the world!

Email has become the communication media of choice. But we must be careful in using this popular means of exchange. Volumes of words can so easily flow off the tips of our fingers.

Then there are those 'forwarded attachments' to consider! The plethora of stories – many recycled four or five times – that fill cyberspace with their 'inspiration'. Many of them are really good. But before you press those two or three keys necessary to rush that message off to your friend, consider these three questions: 1) Is it something that will really minister to a current need in his life? (That answer might come in prayer.) 2) Does he have the time to read yours, and theirs and the others? 3) How much will it cost him to download all those 'cool' graphics and audios? What will the cost be if he loses his connection and has to start downloading over again?

Communicate through photos. Enclose a photo now and then with your letter. A missionary recalls, 'When we were abroad, we had a wall of pictures of friends and family. After all, it was the only place we saw their smiling faces. It was a lingering point for memories and prayer.'

One of the missionary's sending team adds, 'We have our own wall of cork arranged as the continents of the world. Over a hundred pictures (updated as they send new ones) place our missionary friends in their respective countries. It is for us, too, a place for prayer and memories in our house.'

But again, be very careful and sensitive in sending high resolution photos by email. It may be so easy for you, but so expensive for him to receive and download.

Videotaping is inexpensive and offers endless communication possibilities. Videotape your home fellowship meeting. Update your worker with a travelling tour of what's going on in your town. Tape a family gathering. Interview people he knows as they come out of church, and introduce him to the newcomers. Send tapes of special programmes, ceremonies and sermons.

There are excellent Christian videos for children. What you send may be the only video your workers' children can watch since in many countries television is often more explicit than in the UK. There are, of course, good videos for adults as well. Be sure to check with your missionary about the type of video they have; different operating systems are used in different countries. Also, consider the newer forms of recording that your missionary may have access to: CDs, DVDs, digital, MP3 or MP4, and, who knows what will be next!

Send audiotape letters. Just begin talking into the cassette recorder as if you are talking to your friend in person. It is hard at first because there is no feedback. But that barrier of one-way communication can be overcome. And it is refreshing to hear each other's voices as you develop this method of sharing. They can record over the same tape in their response to you.

Send a group audiotape made at a family gathering or an impromptu interview with people as they come out of church: 'Hey, in twenty words or less, what do you want to say to......?' Let your field worker feel part of the home church by recording meetings and get-togethers. Fill their ears with the sounds of the children's choir or crickets chirping or frogs croaking – if that's what they miss.

Provide a website for your missionary friend. There are organizations who will for a small or no fee allow your missionary friend set up a web page. He can provide you (and his whole support team) with any creative communication he has the time to develop.

A 'care' parcel is a great idea. Of course, check first with the post office and with your missionary or society on what may be sent. Find out how to label parcels properly. It is amazing what you can put even in a letter envelope. Find out what your airmail charges plus their duty charges will be; otherwise you might send a parcel that costs double or triple what it is worth.

There are many items that will communicate your love for them: new books, music tapes, Bible study tapes. One cross-cultural worker once mentioned that he really enjoys the Sunday sports section of his local newspaper. A loyal friend now sends it to him every week! From the UK it is possible to arrange for a weekly newspaper to be sent airmail almost anywhere. *The Daily Telegraph* will send *The Weekly Telegraph* and *The Guardian* will send *The Guardian Weekly* for about £1.50 per week. This is much appreciated. Sometimes even the little things that seem like nothing to us – a packet of salad dressing mix or chilli powder – are a delightful surprise if your missionaries live where those items are not available.

But don't be surprised if their tastes have changed. Ask them what their needs and their wants are now. No matter how mundane the request, if it will minister to them, send it!

Personal visits, of course, are the ultimate in communication. How Paul longed to see his support team. And he thanked them profusely when they sent a representative to minister to his needs (see Philippians 4:15–18, for example).

One church takes a group to Israel each year. Their missionaries in Greece and Turkey have the opportunity every other year to spend this time with their friends from home – in Israel! The church pays the missionaries' fares to come from their place of ministry to Israel for these ten days of fellowship and holiday.

The pastor of one church regularly visits the church's missionaries to put a 'new heart' in them and to encourage them in the Lord.

Even if you or someone from your fellowship cannot make the visit, if you know of someone going to your worker's location or nearby, you can encourage that traveller to visit your missionary, and to take a message or parcel of love and concern. On the other hand, if your worker lives at a major crossroads of world travellers, you might need to 'protect' him from being a perpetual host and tour guide!

Communication support is caring and expressing it; caring is communication!

A Case Study in Communication Support

Lou and Sandy's support team makes a special effort to communicate with them:

As my husband and I moved into the home that Lou and Sandy moved out of, we see to their post. Most people send personal mail directly to the Philippines, so we basically collect Lou's magazines, newsletters and other second class mail and a few personal letters that may not be sent directly to them. We mail all of this in a manila envelope once or twice a month, depending on the accumulation. Bank statements, tax returns, bills and other legal papers we hand over to Tim, who is in charge of Logistics Support.

We also send the Sunday sermon tapes in that envelope. Often we include an interesting front page of our local newspaper or Lou's favourite cartoons!

We have also sent care parcels. We try to send special treats for each of them – things that they cannot buy where they live. In each one we include a treat or gift for their host family or the national staff with whom they work.

Because communication is two-way, on one Sunday each month we put up a Philippines mission table. There is an attractive display with updated information about Lou and Sandy and the mission with which they work. At this table we hand out pre-addressed aerogrammes to people who will write that month to Lou and Sandy.

Apparently there has been no lack of letter communication. In one six-week period, they reported, they had gone only three days without at least one letter, and one day they had received seven!

One month Lou (who is interested in statistical analysis) kept track of the postmarks on the mail they received. (That, in itself, tells us they are getting a good amount of mail!)

Lou reported, 'In checking the postmarks from our supporters to see how long it took for the mail to get to us, we noticed a bell curve based on the arrival of our prayer letter to them. Forty-seven per cent of our Communication Support Team sent their letters to us within a week of their receiving our letter! It pays to write and to personalize our letters!'

The ultimate in communication support was afforded Lou and Sandy last summer. Our mission pastor and his family used part of their holiday to visit them in the Philippines. We sent our love along with them in a hundred tangible ways. And they returned our love with thankful hearts.

'Reach out and touch someone', the Bell telephone system used to say. You can still do it through soul-satisfying communication support. But the full circle of supporting your missionary is completed through *re-entry* support as you welcome him back home.

(In addition to the individual study below, see the **Group Leader's Guide** for session six beginning on page 202.)

For your Personal Involvement

- Read one of Paul's letters and highlight all the personal messages and comments. You may be surprised how much of his letters dealt with personal communication, logistics and the desire just to convey his friendship.
- Select one of the other letter-writers in the Bible. Identify the kinds of 'ordinary' things he talked about.

- Check with the mission groups of other churches to discover what specific ideas they use in their communication support.
- Talk with missionaries on furlough. Find out from them the kinds of communication support they receive, which are appreciated most, and why.
- Review the different methods of communication suggested in this chapter. Which are you particularly interested in? Do you have the necessary equipment for that or those methods?

Action Steps

By the time you have read Chapter Six, completed the 'For Your Personal Involvement' section and participated in a discussion group, you should:

- Be able to decide if this is the area of support the Lord is directing you into. If so, get out pen and paper now! Write to that missionary God has put on your heart and post it today.
- Prepare a form for parents and children to complete before they go, telling of their needs and wants. Be sure to include a place for their birthdays and anniversaries, types of books they like, music or study tapes they enjoy. If your missionaries are already overseas send the form to them. When they return it, be sure to follow up regularly at least some of their requests.
- Find out what types of things survive in the mail and what things to avoid sending. Find out costs of parcels of various weights and the approximate time it takes between sending and receiving a parcel.
- Involve others. Actively share what you are doing and look for others who might get involved.

Chapter Seven

Re-entry Support

'And they stayed there a long time with the disciples.'
Acts 14:28

'My father was a career missionary. My brothers and sisters and I were born on the mission field. This was our life. Dad diligently directed a theological college for the whole western region of the country. Mother stood faithfully by his side. Our education was as much enhanced by watching their lives as it was by the lessons in our classrooms.

'Through the years they had weathered any number of the storms that assail missionaries. Each brought them to a more determined level of commitment to our Lord and to the cause of training national leaders.

'Tensions between national Christians and missionary leaders were frequent. But my dad was a peacemaker. He could walk that delicate line of cultural sensitivity. Lack of funds became so common that we all knew when to "tighten our belts". Discouragement over "promising" national students who turned their backs on Christian service only toughened Dad's resolve to pour his life into others.

137

'But probably the most trying experience Dad and Mum faced was the uncertain life or death outcome of his arrest during a military coup. With all the drama of a war film, soldiers barged into our house and took Dad prisoner. They were sure he had secret contacts with the enemies of the people.

'The coup failed. After three weeks Dad was released and resumed his work at the college.

'We kids are grown up now. Several of us are married and back on the mission field ourselves.

'But last summer Dad called us all together for a family meeting. By the curtness of the invitation and his insistence on our being there, we could tell something was wrong. In a thousand years we would never have dreamed of what was to take place. The meeting was short and to the point. In essence: "Children, it is important for you to know that I am divorcing your mother. I plan to marry Sue." Sue is younger than I am! His parting words were, "And furthermore, I'm not even sure there is a God."'

In the secular world they are saying it: re-entry is often the hardest part of an overseas experience and it should not be ignored. There are unexpected problems in returning home. Family members who have lived in another culture need to learn how to overcome the difficulties of today's workplace, community and school environments.

In the Christian community they are saying it: up to 50 per cent of first-time missionaries return home early or don't return for a second term. These wounded people need to identify and process the hurt and anger of failure – to begin to build up their lives again, growing toward mental and spiritual wholeness.

In missions seminars they are saying it. One leader emphasized, 'I have not led one seminar about the acute need for re-entry help without some missionary coming to me and saying, "I thought I was weird. I couldn't tell anyone about my feelings. Thank you for letting me know that it is OK to feel a little uncomfortable in coming home."

'Recently, just as I finished the re-entry session of a seminar, a woman in the front began sobbing, then weeping uncontrollably. Finally, through her tears, she wailed, "I have been home from Indonesia for three months. Everything you just talked about I am experiencing. Please help me!"'

The Situation of Re-entry

There is an initial *shock* in returning home. Old buildings have been torn down; new ones have taken their place. A favourite park is now a busy traffic junction. Grandma's chair is empty. Your cross-cultural worker probably heard about all these things as they happened. But now that he is home and sees them for himself, he's shaken. These factors however are gradually absorbed and accepted.

The *stress* of coming home is another issue. There is a mental stretching as new ideas and ideals are incorporated into the old – which isn't old anymore since that too is new and strangely different.

There is a spiritual duress caused by the continual memory of the needs of a world lost in sin and what we are or aren't doing about those needs.

There is physical stress as well-meaning people gorge their newly returned missionary with junk foods. 'You're so skinny; have some more!'

There are odd emotions as perhaps your missionary tries to justify the new and expensive wardrobe of clothes that has just been graciously given him. Days before he left, his national partner had refused to accept a shirt from him with the words, 'I have one to wear while I wash the other. A third one would just be wasted!'

Yes, the home scene with its people, places, and things – all that you represent – has changed. But more dramatically, your missionary friend has changed – socially, emotionally, mentally, physically and most of all spiritually. And because these changes happened to each of you so gradually, you yourselves are only slightly aware of them. But as you meet, the changes in each other appear drastic!

Needless to say, the longer your cross-cultural worker has been away, the more pronounced will be the culture stress in coming home.

But even short assignments can produce dramatically bold changes. A zealous Pharisee named Saul was on a mission. In that foriegn land of Syria, he was riding toward Damascus. In the span of a few minutes, his entire life was changed. In a blinding light, his eyes were opened! (Read Acts 9:1–20.)

In many situations of world need today, God can instantly open your missionary's eyes to crying needs for ministry. Short-term mission trainers report, 'For simple exposure to another culture, we have taken people across the border into France and watched God break their hearts with compassion for the lost and needy of this world, in just one afternoon.'

There is another factor to consider in re-entry support: denial. Some workers may prepare to return home denying that they will face any stress upon re-entry. Some steel themselves with the attitude that 'it won't – it can't happen to me.'

Denial can be suicide – emotional, spiritual, mental. And even literal, physical suicide has been the result of some missionaries' shock and stress in re-entry. Your returning missionary may think, 'Look how easy it was for me to adjust to my new culture on the field. What's the big deal? I'm just going home!'

Look at some possible blind spots in that statement:

1) The adaptation probably wasn't as easy as he now remembers it;
2) The months (maybe years) of anticipation before going gave him time to prepare for the adjustments;
3) The nationals of the host culture may have been accustomed to Westerners and therefore knew how to help him adapt. In many cultures the people are very gentle, non-demanding and forgiving of missionaries.

None of those factors will cushion his re-entry as he comes home. Perhaps his unaware friends back home are echoing the same words: 'What's the big deal? He's just coming home!' Because many of them have not ventured beyond the comfort zones of their own world, they have no idea of what a missionary goes through in living and ministering in a second culture. Many supporters feel coming home is basically a non-issue.

Awareness of the factors of re-entry can prepare you to become a strongly supportive friend in the 'coming home' process.

The Challenge of Re-entry

As a re-entry support person, it is necessary for you to keep your eyes and ears open for signs of culture stress in reverse. The returning field worker is the one least prepared to handle the situation. He knows something's not right! The loneliness, the disappointment and let-down, feelings of isolation and not belonging here, the dizzying speeds of everything may find him silently crying, 'Slow down! Slow down!' But it doesn't slow down.

You must take the initiative. You must be the 'intensive care unit' for your missionary's re-entry.

He will face challenges of re-entry in any one or more of the following areas:

1) Physically

We joke about jet lag: jet lag is the process of making you look like your passport photo! But it is a serious issue that can last for several days. The physical challenge that your returning missionary friend may experience goes beyond jet lag. If he has ministered at an elevation greatly different than the one to which he returns, adjustment time is needed. Climatic conditions, such as moving from hot to cold regions or humid to dry areas do not allow for immediate adjustment. Seasonal changes experienced by returning from the Southern Hemisphere to the Northern may give your friend a difficult adjustment. You need to help your friend (and others who understand the action) that it is all right to reach for a jumper in hot weather when he has just returned from the humid rain forests of Peru to the temperate zone of south London.

2) Professionally

After the adventure of an overseas experience, going back to his old job could be very boring. Equally perplexing could be the 'big-fish-in-a-little-pond' syndrome. Upon return, he suddenly becomes a small-to-medium-sized-fish in a much bigger pond! He may lament, 'The light of my testimony looked so much brighter out there where it was dark!' Or he may feel the loss of some degree of independence as he is now under the more watchful eye of his employer. Or the feeling of being in the old rat race may begin to haunt him.

In some areas of work, a year or two away may mean the former job is obsolete. One woman working in computers realized this during her training before she went overseas as a short-termer. Helping her through that stress before she left made re-entry easier for her later. In fact, when she returned, she said, 'I'm not going back into computers. I am working at a nursing home. I see this as a ministry now, and the medical training I'm getting will really open up new opportunities for me to go again where workers are needed.'

3) Materially-Financially

The country your worker is coming back to is generally much more expensive. That doesn't mean that a loaf of bread necessarily costs more. It does mean that the British spend more money on things than the people of the culture from which he is returning.

When your cross-cultural workers return to this, it may cause stress! When they see a teenager go to a full wardrobe of clothes and cry, 'I haven't got anything to wear!' they remember the hours they struggled over how to ask people at home for extra money to feed and clothe local children.

One recently returned missionary said, 'The wealth of this country is very difficult to handle; the wealth of the church is even more difficult for me to deal with.'

Another missionary said, 'It happened to my wife this way: a few months after our return from Mozambique, she was leisurely walking the aisles of a supermarket, choosing this, and wisely picking that off the shelves. All of a sudden, she felt overwhelmed. She began thinking, "There are too many choices. I have to get out of here!" She left her half-full trolley there in the aisle, went to the car and drove home!'

Another recalled, 'In Brazil, owing to our various economic and living conditions, personal ownership took a back seat in our minds. Upon our arrival home, I began working with a fellow who was using a new pen. They had not been on the market when we left. He let me use it. I commented to him how I enjoyed the feel of it and how good the writing looked.

'The next day he gave me one. "Here, this is yours!" For several days, I would pause and just look at that treasure. "It's mine! It's really mine!" I would muse to myself.'

'Ridiculous!' you might say. Yes, but this is the very level on which culture stress in reserve occurs.

Comparative wealth can begin the stress even before your missionaries leave the field. And children are susceptible as well as adults: Bill and Alice were houseparents in a children's home for Wycliffe Bible Translators in the northern Philippines. Their son William had had an opportunity to spend a week in a tribal village.

Sometime after his return to the Wycliffe Centre, Alice saw William looking into his clothes closet. He was crying. Knowing her own concern for how little they had compared to their lifestyle at home she went to console him. After several attempts at resisting her comfort, he said, 'No, Mum. I feel sad that I have so much in comparison to my new friends in the tribe.'

4) Culturally

New beliefs, values, attitudes and behaviour patterns have become a part of your returning worker. Perhaps he has adjusted to a culture with a slower pace, a more relaxed atmosphere, an emphasis on people and relationships, different foods, an afternoon siesta.

The cultural differences that your returning missionary may try to hold onto are innumerable. When schedules and attitudes of people here at home now don't allow for them, he feels irritation and stress!

One major expectation of most returnees is that people will be interested in their experiences: 'We had been invited to their house for the evening,' one returning missionary wrote. 'We assumed it was to be able to share the excitement of our missionary venture. After a delicious meal during which we were able to insert a few comments, we were ushered into the family room. "Now is our opportunity," I thought. But as our host turned on the TV, he said, "I was sure you would enjoy watching our new 29-inch screen!" I was absolutely devastated!'

What a different story is told of the Antioch church welcoming home their travel-weary pioneer missionaries: 'From Attalia they sailed back to Antioch where they had been committed to the grace of God for the work they had now completed. On arriving there, they gathered the church together and reported all that God had done through them and how he had opened the door of faith to the Gentiles' (Acts 14:26, 27).

5) Socially

Many people place a missionary on a spiritual pedestal. 'How can we relate with someone who has been a missionary?' they wonder. 'What would we talk about?'

Or some may fear that the missionary is infectious. 'If I have them over for dinner, will my children catch some kind of exotic disease?' Worse! 'Their enthusiasm for missions might rub off on me!'

It might seem to returning missionaries that everyone is constantly hurrying hither and thither. After spending some time here, one perceptive international observed: 'Here, everyone has a watch, but no one has any time. In our country, few have watches, but everybody has time!'

Compared to much of the rest of the world, life in the West is extremely busy. When your missionary went abroad, his old friends closed the gap created in their lives by his departure. Social ties may have been broken with time. Former friends' children have made new friends. Family members may have moved away.

If communication between the missionary and his home church has not been good or if it is a particularly large church, he may not even have been missed! One returning missionary who had spent two years of fruitful labour in Europe was greeted by her pastor with, 'Hi, Sally! How was Hawaii?'

One short-term missionary, after returning from a five-week ministry, was welcomed back at church with, 'Bill! You're back! We thought you had backslidden.' It was a blow for the returning missionary since it meant he hadn't being prayed for while on his mission. And if they really thought he had backslidden, why weren't they out looking for him?

There are real situations that may cause stress, but there are also imaginary ones that can be equally distressing. A family recently returned home to their church which had been kept informed about their mission. The husband said, 'My best friends went sailing by, barely saying hello as if I had only been away for a long weekend. I was mortified! I was distraught!' His friends meant no harm. But rejection, whether real or imagined, can have equal consequences.

6) Linguistically

Your returning missionary has probably learned a second language – or at least some phrases. There are many languages far more descriptive than English. He may try to express himself in our limited vocabulary and feel inadequate. Stress! He may have forgotten certain English words – which may seem humorous or inconsequential to most of his listeners. Stress! Some of his responses might automatically come out in his second language. Stress!

Further, colloquialisms and slang have changed. Teenagers of returning families might especially feel stressed by not knowing which words are in or out – or even if 'in' and 'out' are in or out! When you see a puzzled look on your returning friend's face, it may be the stress of not understanding current English!

7) Nationally, Politically

New leadership can bring new laws. As our country increasingly embraces a pluralistic society, a returning missionary could experience stress, wondering under which god our nation stands.

What happens to our nationalistic pride when we discover that Britain, a supposedly Christian country fades into the distance when we see the fervour and devotion of African believers who have so little materially yet so much spiritually?

Having seen the other side of British foreign policy, your missionary's political outlook on this country may be affected. Possibly your returning worker found the life of his host country more to his liking.

As a returned worker simply reads a newspaper editorial about issues now facing his own society, he may feel out of touch with current affairs. And that is when you as a re-entry support 'specialist' (really just a friend) need to have your eyes and ears open!

8) Educationally

The formal and informal educational standards of the world vary. Missionary children may for years have been educated at home or at a boarding school away from their parents. When they now have to go to a large state school, parents can understandably be concerned. The children themselves can feel they are in a potentially devastating situation educationally as well as socially.

One girl, returning from abroad described her first day at school in her home country. 'We circled the monstrous wood and brick building. We surged forward, carried irresistibly toward its mouth and stopped momentarily at its gaping door ... I was now in the monster's throat. I felt a downward, sinking feeling. I was being swallowed! The noise was like thunder ... I was alone in the blackness of that nightmare.'

That description might fit what your returning missionaries and their children all sense during the weeks and months of re-entry.

9) Spiritually

Your returning cross-cultural worker's life has concentrated on the salvation and discipling of the nations, knowing God is 'not wanting anyone to perish but everyone to come to repentance' (2 Peter 3:9). He has become disentangled from the affairs of this world – 'he wants to please his commanding officer' (2 Timothy 2:4). He remembers the cry of the widow, the orphan, the lost and dying.

And now in bold, stark contrast, the demands of a 'godless Christian' society surround him with stress. He is enjoying the pleasures of new conveniences at home in the UK, yet even that enjoyment can create feelings of bewilderment, anger, guilt and condemnation. The hurt is not only for himself; it is also for the hundreds of people he left in his adopted country who need food and care and Bibles and Bible studies and the multitude of other blessings of the West.

Each of these areas – from physical to spiritual factors – is a stress point needing your re-entry support.

Re-entry Behaviour Patterns

Generally speaking there are five different patterns of return behaviour that could show up in your missionary friend. Four of them are dangerous. You need to be alert to the symptoms and help your friend process his feelings, working toward the expression of the fifth pattern. That is the one you need to facilitate. By focusing on it, your friend will be less likely to fall into one of the others.

1) Alienation

The cross-cultural worker comes home. His attitude of 'I'm only going home!' has left him unprepared for what he is facing. He begins feeling very negative about his home culture. Not knowing how to handle what he sees and feels, he begins to withdraw.

He makes excuses rather than meeting people. 'I haven't got my slides together yet,' he says. So he can't share with the home group. 'The crowd at the football match would be too noisy,' he argues. Three weeks later he is still 'suffering from jet lag.' These are the types of symptoms you must be on the look out for. They are shallow pretexts to hide his inner feelings.

He might internalize these feelings and sink further into this pattern of alienation. He may feel there is no one to talk to, no one who could possibly understand; no one to help him process his thoughts.

You can pull him out of that by inviting him to your home. Just the two of you – or three – is a small, safe number. Or visit some of his favourite spots together – a park, a beach, a restaurant. If he refuses all of this, get desperate! Just arrive on his doorstep and insist on some fellowship. Get him talking about anything, so that he begins to verbalize his thoughts.

2) Condemnation

This person is also negative about his home culture. The areas of challenge seem to be overwhelming. He didn't realize people would be so unthinking. He can't understand why his pastor has no time for him. How could they be so unchristian? The pressure of his judgemental attitude increases, and he becomes explosive. Everyone he sees knows within minutes how inferior and lacking in spiritual gifts they are – so he thinks – because they are not involved in missions. He begins to condemn and criticize everything from the church pews to Mrs Brown's new hairstyle.

Be blunt about his condemnation. Because he is so forcefully verbalizing his criticisms, it may cause you to become defensive. Don't allow it! Remember, this is *his* problem. Let him talk to you. Help him deal with these issues before they develop roots of bitterness (Hebrews 12:15). He, too, needs to process all his frustrations in a safe environment of a close friendship. Don't wait until he feels he must unload in the middle of a church meeting.

3) Reversion

This person takes a hop, skip and a jump off the plane only to discover people aren't hopping, skipping and jumping any more. Yet he keeps trying to deny that any vital changes took place in him while he was gone, or in you who stayed at home. He keeps trying to fit in to what was but no longer is.

This person is likely to jump right into whatever task is put before him. And his unaware friends play right into this dilemma: 'So glad you're back! We need a teacher for the sixth form class!' 'Great! When do I start?' Usher? 'Yes, I will!' Lead worship on Wednesday night? 'Of course!'

He will wake up one morning doubting his sanity. He has moved into the fast lane of Western Christianity without allowing time to process the incredible changes his body, soul and spirit have undergone.

4) The Ultimate Escape

Alienation, condemnation or reversion could lead your cross-cultural worker into a devastating scenario of the ultimate escape of suicide – figurative or actual.

The missionary went out to live and minister in a second culture. He had a good experience. Language was learned. Relationships were nurtured. Souls were saved. The church was strengthened.

He returns. He is not prepared for the changes at home. He tries to cope. He internalizes all his frustrations. Alienation whispers, 'Nobody cares or understands. Forget them!' He argues with himself, 'No, I have to get out and share a vision for the world among the church people.' 'But they are so ungodly,' condemnation thunders. 'This isn't getting me anywhere,' he yells back at himself. Reversion reasons, 'OK, let's just forget it. I was there. You were here. We're back together. No big deal!'

The whirlwind of emotions leaves him broken. He backs out of life – spiritually, mentally, emotionally, or finds the ultimate escape his only alternative.

If you see your returning friend falling into any one of these four behaviour patterns, your help is needed.

The most vital immediate help you can give is to listen. Take the time to hear his heart, to share his experiences, to care about his feelings and burdens, to see his slides, to be there when he needs someone to talk and laugh and cry with.

Reunion parties are fine. But what about at three in the morning: you're awakened by the phone. At first you don't hear anyone on the line. Then you hear someone softly sobbing. You say, 'Suzie, is that you?' There's a weak, hardly distinguishable, 'yes.' You say, 'I'll be with you as soon as I can!'

Let her say anything in the confidence of your friendship. Don't interject, 'I know, yes, I understand.' You probably don't. Just let her talk. Encourage her to keep talking by asking leading questions to explain something she had referred to. Ask 'And how did you feel when that happened?' Affirm with, 'That must have been tough/terrifying/exciting/etc.'

Because you've been sensitive to your friend's re-entry needs, you have helped them avoid these negative behaviour patterns. Therefore, you can help them focus on a fifth return behaviour pattern – the only healthy one.

It bears repeating: by *initially* focusing on this one, the others are more likely to be avoided:

5) Integration

Helping your missionary integrate takes place on two levels: immediate and long-term.

The Immediate

a) Be sure your workers are welcomed and picked up at the airport. Don't overwhelm them with half the church being there, but a good-sized group who will say, 'We're glad you're home!' One church welcoming party arrived at the airport two days after the missionary had come home. Fortunately his parents had confirmed the correct day of his arrival and were there to meet him!

b) Arrange somewhere for them to stay. 'And (Paul and Barnabas) stayed there a long time' (Acts 14:28). There are twelve Greek words we can use to translate 'stay', and it is interesting to note that the one used here can be defined as to wear through by rubbing; to rub away! In other words, their stay with the disciples in Antioch was of such a duration that all strangeness of relationship had come to be 'rubbed away'. When you stay with someone, you know where the extra light bulbs are stored. You aren't just camping out in their house. Whether it is with friends, family, or in a place of their own, be sure to check with your missionaries before they return. Prepare them for the accommodation you are providing for them.

As a church recently welcomed home their first missionary family, the pastor said, 'The washing machine and tumbled-dryer are installed, the water and electricity are on, the fridge is full, the telephone's connected. I think we're ready!'

c) Have some immediate means of transport for them – a borrowed car or a dependable, inexpensive one that can be sold when they return overseas. One returning woman said, 'Not only did they have a comfortable, dependable car available for my three months at home, but a petrol card for me to use.' It is important that returning missionaries have some independence and the freedom to be mobile.

d) Provide meals for the first few days. Invite them over; take food in; equip them with some basic food supplies – and maybe a few treats. But be sensitive. Don't make it difficult for them to say no. Some missionaries have said, 'I can hardly wait to get back to the field. I won't have to eat so much!'

e) Take them shopping. They may not know what styles are fashionable. And they can look conspicuously out of place without even knowing it. Care must be taken here also, as your friend may have learned to dress more conservatively and to manage with fewer clothes.

f) Perhaps they had a complete medical check-up before leaving. If not, ask them if they would appreciate you making arrangements for doctor, dental and eye care visits – free or discounted or paid for by you or the church.

g) After an appropriate few days have a get-together – perhaps a bring and share dinner – so that they can meet more people in a shorter time. A ladies' tea is great for the women to catch up and feel part of things again. But again, be sensitive. They may want to spend most of their time alone for the first week or so.

h) Remember the children; they have personal needs too.

Long Term Interaction

Help returned missionaries to integrate their new identity and lifestyle slowly into their new environment. They have the opportunity and challenge to be positive change agents – people who can purposefully help all of you at home to see the world more and more from God's perspective. Be open to their new ideas and ways of doing things.

Allow the creative genius of God to expand your thinking to other ways your missionaries can share their experiences. You can thereby facilitate a good debriefing for them. Paul and Barnabas, on their arrival in Antioch, were given the opportunity to gather 'the church together and reported all that God had done through them and how he had opened the door of faith to the Gentiles' (Acts 14:27).

Look for creative ways to help your missionary introduce global perspectives to your friends. What groups of people could you interest in hearing his report: Sunday school classes? Home groups? Prayer groups? Schools? Other church groups? Local radio or TV? A newspaper article? Is their story worth writing about? Could you put video clips on a CD-Rom for him to use as he travels?

Listen to hear what God has done in his life. Allow him to keep everything in perspective as he readjusts to his home culture.

Scripture further says of Paul and Barnabas that they stayed in Antioch for some time teaching and preaching the Word of the Lord (Acts 15:35). In other words, the time came when they picked up the ministry they had been involved in before going. In its time – if they are not returning overseas – taking up a ministry in the church would be a goal for your cross-cultural workers. This might possibly be in their area of previous ministry. But it is also possible that with their cross-cultural ministry experience, they would now be suited to further develop your church's involvement with people from other countries who are living among you. Or to train new missionary recruits. Or to develop the many aspects of strong sending teams.

Personalizing Re-entry Support

There may be special re-entry concerns for various members of the family:

1) Husbands can need help

As a family returns from the field, there are pressures and anxious feelings of responsibility for the husband as provider. Financial support may have dropped because they aren't abroad now. Yet expenses are probably higher here at home.

Take the initiative in talking about money. Maybe you can help financially, maybe not. But you have helped by broaching the subject. Even that may help to sort out priorities. And, then again, it might bring a totally new, Holy Spirit-inspired solution.

Go easy with this, but the time will come to help him talk about future plans. 'What career are you going to pursue?' 'Are you planning to go back to college?' 'Overseas?' 'Back to your previous employment?'

2) Behind every good man is a great wife!

On the mission field she probably played a much more active role in ministry than she will now. Be sure to allow opportunities for her to share. If this is not appropriate in your public gatherings, provide occasions in your living room. The wife in the missionary team has often experienced enormous pressures in the balance of ministry and family affairs, and her needs to share are equally valid.

She is pleased with the fully-carpeted, three-bedroom house the church has rented for them. But she is at a loss to know how she is going to keep it clean. More often than not overseas she had a maid who had helped even with the cooking! Help her ease back into the way of life here. Be willing to help her with it for a time.

3) Missionary kids are ordinary kids

Born to British parents but brought up in Japan, Zaire, Cairo or Hong Kong, missionary kids (MKs) often don't know where they fit in. The UK is their homeland, but it usually isn't their home.

A 14-year-old MK, after returning overseas from a year at home wrote an essay entitled, *What I would like to tell people at home.*

I want to answer a few questions I have been asked: No! We don't live in mud huts. No! We don't eat foreign food. It is very natural. MKs are not perfect. We're human and have faults and virtues like everybody else. When you subconsciously or otherwise treat us as if we should be perfect, we get bawled out by you (who have no right at all) and then by our parents (who know better).

No! All MKs are not super brats. Those few who act like it on furlough are probably trying to hide the culture shock they are going through. No! Just because you're an MK doesn't mean you know your Bible any better than anyone else. All the time when we were on furlough, I was asked to quote Scripture or find something in the Bible I had never heard of. People were shocked and whispered behind their hands.

No! MKs don't go around barefoot and in rags. Mrs X had seen a picture of me in a paint-spotted t-shirt and cut offs and assumed I didn't have anything better to wear. Please send money! The money sent to missionaries is never enough! Even though it often appears as if my parents aren't doing anything, they are! And our national friends will tell you so!

How can you support a returning MK? Employ with an MK all the tenderness, understanding, tact, wisdom and patience you would use in being a re-entry support person for an adult.

4) Single and satisfied!

This phrase (the title and subject of a book) might remind senders that single people need special re-entry support, too. Few married people understand single ministry workers' needs of being cared for. And few married couples realize the unintentional insensitivity and hurt hurled at single adults in even Christian circles.

Sometimes re-entry is harder for a single person. At least family members have each other to talk to. Loneliness, perplexities, inability to cope with modern single relationships and the desire to get on with life can throw unmarried returned missionaries into states of alienation and depression. You can be there to draw them out! Be there to listen and serve.

We are the body of Christ. We are a community of believers. We need each other. May God challenge you to become part of a Re-entry Support Team who are serving as senders!

A Case Study in Re-entry Support

One of the senders team we've been following in our case studies reports:

> My wife Teri and I are the core group leaders of re-entry support for Lou and Sandy. The only experience we have in this was the short time Lou and Sandy were with us between their field training in Mexico and actually going to the Philippines. Because their time in Mexico was only three months, there didn't seem to be any of the major culture shock or stress problems. Still, when they came back from Mexico, we tried to make things as normal as possible for them. This was good practise for us!
>
> Oddly enough the process started before they left for their field training. It began with a commitment on their part to keep those of us at home informed of what was going on in their lives in Mexico. We were kept up-to-date on prayer needs and trying situations in their training and in their new culture. We were told about the victories and the defeats. They kept us informed about their daughter Marlies and how she was growing and how all of them were adjusting to living with their Mexican host family. A key to this communication was that it was regular. We were with them as they progressed through the twelve weeks.
>
> And that paid off. When they got home they didn't have to feel pressured to condense or just hit the highlights of their experiences. And we hadn't missed so many of the little things that had contributed to who they now were. There was already a group of us who had gone through it with them, families with whom they could feel comfortable in rehashing some of their experiences. This detailed debriefing proved as important to them as it was informative to us.

Another aspect of their re-entry support was to attend to their physical needs. Before Lou and Sandy left for Mexico, they had sold most of their household goods and had left their home. So they needed a place to stay for about seven weeks until their departure for the Philippines. Initially there was the chance that they might be able to house-sit for a family that was going to be out of town. As that hope faded and eventually disappeared, Teri and I felt that we should open our home to them. Many factors contributed to our volunteering. We already knew them well and knew that our lifestyles were compatible. The Lord had blessed us with a house large enough for eight to live in comfortably (including a kitchen large enough for both Teri and Sandy). There was an extra room that could be just for Lou and Sandy, while Marlies could sleep in our daughter's room. And, most importantly, we all prayed about it and felt that the Lord was saying, 'Yes!'

We were aware that a lot of people might want to spend some time with Lou and Sandy before they left for the Philippines, so we planned a bring and share lunch after church on their first Sunday home from Mexico.

Because we knew that there were quite a number of their friends who would like to share a meal or spend an evening with them, we decided to keep an appointment/social calendar so that they could budget their time. We prepared a letter that was sent to the other core group members and all support members expressing Lou and Sandy's desire to spend time with those who wished to visit. It also explained their need for time to take care of unfinished business and to relax. The letter was sent out well in advance of their return. Teri acted as their appointments secretary. Lou gave us directions on how full to make their calendar and what days they already had planned for other things.

The rest was simply working with the people who phoned so that everyone could spend some time with them.

It made things easier for us and even more enjoyable for Lou and Sandy when we could get a couple of families together at the same time. The letter proved to be successful in that Lou and Sandy were able to accomplish their three goals of seeing people, going over business matters and relaxing.

The room we were able to provide for them was our den. We rearranged the furniture, brought in a bed and a chest of drawers and put a lock on the door so they could have privacy. They had their own keys to our house so they could come and go as they pleased. Even though they still had their own car, they were free also to use one of ours when they went in different directions.

We have lived with other people at various times during our marriage, but I don't remember it ever being so tension-free. I think the major factor in this good living situation was that Lou and Sandy were doing exactly what God wanted them to do in preparing for the mission field and we as Re-entry Support Team were doing exactly what God wanted us to do. He had prepared all of us to live together – for a while at least. And, as the widow from Zarephath who provided hospitality for Elijah found, the Spirit of God rested on our house.

Though our task will be greater when Lou and Sandy return on furlough, we have learned a lot from this experience. Re-entry support doesn't begin when the cross-cultural worker returns home. It starts before they leave. It continues while they are gone. And accelerates when they return. While they are in the Philippines we are keeping in close contact with them so that when they return there will be a group of us who are not cultural strangers to them. We will be able immediately to relate to them as they begin their debriefing.

This then is the full circle of support you can offer to your cross-cultural worker as you express your love and concern for him while he is preparing to go, while he is on the field and when he returns home.

Subsequent to the writing of this book, I have had numerous opportunities to share these principles of missionary care. Soon I became aware that re-entry was the least understood of the six areas.

I took to the task of writing a book dealing specifically with care at this most critical time in the life of a missionary: *The Re-entry Team: Caring for your Returning Missionaries.* In Section One, I present the biblical model and the human dilemma that makes it so difficult to follow that so simply stated five-step model. Section Two contains seventy stories written by returned missionaries. Each one is followed by a bit of commentary and action steps to help the reader avoid the pitfalls of the negative experience and emulate the success of the positive stories. (This resource is available through OSCAR. Contact Mike Frith at mike@oscar.org.uk)

(In addition to the individual study below, see the **Group Leader's Guide** for session seven beginning on page 204.)

For Your Personal Involvement

- Though this aspect of missions life has been long neglected, articles are beginning to appear on the subject. From various missionary magazines collect and read as much as you can about re-entry.
- Talk with missionaries who are on furlough or those who have returned permanently about the challenge of re-entry. But be prepared for some tears! Many missionaries, unless they have had a good Re-entry Support Team, have a lot of bottled-up emotions.

- As you listen to these people, try to identify symptoms of the first four re-entry behaviour patterns.
- Write to the missionary societies of your cross-cultural workers. Ask them for the materials and useful ideas they recommend to help when missionaries return home.
- Write to other missionary societies and ask them for their materials and procedures. Learn all you can about this needy area of missionary support.

Action Steps

By the time you have read Chapter Seven, completed the 'For Your Personal Involvement section' and participated in a discussion group, you should:

- Be able to decide if this is the area of support the Lord is directing you into.
- If it is, write to the missionary God has placed on your heart. Ask him if this is OK with him. Find out if there are others who have made this commitment to him. Begin discussions about responsibilities with the others.
- Four months before your cross-cultural worker comes home, send him material collected on re-entry that will help him prepare for his major transition.
- Buy *The Re-entry Team*. Read and apply it.
- Involve others. Share the material you collect and all you learn about re-entry with others. Make these people aware of this badly neglected area of missionary support.

Chapter Eight

Your Part in the Big Picture

'Be strong and courageous.'
Joshua 1:9

'With tears in her eyes she said, 'I have never heard of this Jesus. Thank you for telling me.' This was the response of our hotel maid as she received a Bible and the message of Christ's love. Before we left, she bowed her head to receive Him as Saviour.

'Little did I realize this story and a story yet unfolding would be birthed as I watched our three-member mission team fly off to our church's adopted people group without me because I had forgotten my passport! As I sat alone in a hotel near JFK airport, I cried out to God. I felt I had failed the Lord, my congregation and my family. But God had a plan. He revealed that night, and in the days to come that our small church family would be used by Him to reach an entire nation with the gospel, but not without Him!

'Our church's involvement began five years before, when six people registered for the "Perspectives" course. During that time we began praying for a couple who were teaching English in a Muslim country which had only one known believer. As the missions committee and church elders prayed, God led us to formally "adopt" this people group.

'On that first trip, after catching up to the other three in our team, I received a deep, God-given love for the people. Through the help of a "tentmaker" Christian worker, I was able to lead a Basketball Clinic for a university team. Because of the one-day delay (due to the forgotten passport), I flew with two Middle Eastern coaches which resulted in an invitation to bring a team from the USA!

'More prayer and another trip! This time we took an Athletes in Action basketball team, which resulted in the establishment of an International Tournament among these Muslim nations. We asked our translator if we should publicly share Christ since it had apparently not been done here for a thousand years! He answered, "The President says we have religious freedom, so do it!"

'During the opening ceremonies, the nation's Vice President asked me to give a greeting. I stepped to the microphone and gave the gym and national TV audience a three-minute gospel message. During our eight-game, two-country tour, we openly preached Christ, resulting in over a hundred declaring their salvation in Christ and hundreds more asking for help and materials.

'After returning home, we learned that each of the five churches in the capital had been closed down by the police. Our church prayed and fasted. God not only changed the leaders' hearts to reopen the churches, but our team was invited for a Second Annual Tournament.

'In preparation for this second basketball outreach, our church family and other friends prepared, prayed and fasted, and gave financially for the trip. However, in the week prior to leaving, one of the players broke his ankle, several players were unable to secure their financial support, one of the two tournaments was cancelled, and officials told us we would not be able to share Christ openly. When it seemed impossible, God provided another player, the finances, an extended stay in our adopted country, and a game in a neighbouring country.

'The spiritual battle was still being fought as we arrived. We could not share Christ during the intervals as we had been told. But the officials also turned off all the lights immediately after our games so that we could not talk with the people. We sent urgent email messages home. And God intervened!

'In answer to those prayers, a member of the President's cabinet invited me to his office. This began a chain of events that encompasses international exchange on government and university levels, international oil and telecommunication companies, leaders of Christian moral and ethics curriculum development and multi-million dollar agreements. Without giving details (because negotiations are in progress), we can say that God has fulfilled not only what He had revealed to me in that lonely hotel room, but has done far more than we could imagine! And the story continues!'

Why is it so crucial that you and your fellowship are strong and courageous to serve as senders? Because God is orchestrating a concert of global activity in our times in which tens of thousands of new missionaries are going to every people, tribe, tongue and nation. And every goer needs a solid team of senders. You and your 'little church' could reach a nation – and nations – for Christ! In the section that follows we look at the work of the missionary organization Operation Mobilization (OM), and their part in the 'big picture'.

OM's Part in the Big Picture

A glance at statistics tells us that OM is 4,080 adults from more than 90 nationalities serving together in over 100 countries and on two ocean-going ships, the LOGOS II and DOULOS (with a third, LOGOS HOPE, undergoing a major refit before it starts service as the replacement for LOGOS II).

But as you get to know them better you'll see that OM is an international, interdenominational movement of Christians committed to partnership with the church of Jesus Christ for the evangelization of the world through biblical teaching, a lifestyle of personal holiness and spiritual reality, and by sending out international evangelistic teams who have had some cross-cultural training.

From this diversity of background, wherever you are with OM, one thing is sure – you will see them doing evangelism. Many different methods are used, like literature distribution, drama, coffee bars, children's meetings, open-air outreach, concerts, friendship-building and more. Whatever the method, the goal is to share the good news of God's love.

OM traces its roots to one woman in northern New Jersey who prayed for fifteen years that God would save local high school students and that some of those who found the Lord would become missionaries.

One day she sent a copy of the Gospel of John to a teenager. Three years later, George Verwer, that young man, gave his life to Jesus Christ. In 1957, during their school holiday, George, Dale Rhoton and Walter Borchard drove to Mexico with 15,000 Spanish Gospels in an old lorry. Christian bookshops, radio broadcasts, and the first OM full-time worker – a Mexican – resulted.

Since Operation Mobilization founder George Verwer and three companions went on their first outreach in

Mexico in 1957, tens of thousands of men and women have served with this missions movement. Thousands of OM alumni now serve as missionaries and pastors, and over one hundred missions have been formed by former OM workers.

As mentioned already, over 4,000 serve with OM in over 100 nations, including young men and women in the initial stages of training and service, seasoned cross-cultural church planters, and professionals offering technical skills in service to the Lord and OM's global ministries.

In earlier years OM helped break new ground, mobilizing missionary sending from the growing churches of Asia, Africa, and Latin America. Today over 60 per cent of OMers are from non-Western countries. A Korean is the Director of OM's ship DOULOS, one of 170 OMers from his homeland. OM's largest ministry is found in India, with over 1,500 Indians serving, many cross-culturally, to reach their nation and its many peoples. Across Central and South Asia and the Middle East, in places where until recently Christians were few, national Christians are joining the ranks of OM, some as senior leaders, to reach their own nations and beyond.

OM is passionately striving to mobilize God's people across the globe for world evangelization with special concern for Europe, the Middle East and Central Asia, the Indian subcontinent and the port cities of the world. For more information about Operation Mobilization's ministries, needs, and opportunities for service contact your national OM office (see the list of addresses on page 188) or visit OM's international website at www.om.org.

Look What God is Doing

Why is it so crucial that you and your fellowship gear up to serve as senders? Because most world Christians believe God is beginning a surge of global activity in our times in which tens of thousands of new missionaries will be going to every people, tribe, tongue and nation. And every goer will need a solid, committed team of senders.

Commenting on the challenge ahead in the twenty-first century, George Verwer, founder of Operation Mobilization, said:

> I am convinced that by a work of the Holy Spirit, God has given us the privilege of being on the cutting edge of reaching unreached peoples. We are daily challenged to stay on the fine line of what God is doing in the world. There is, of course, also great opposition. As Paul wrote to the Christians in Corinth, 'a great door for effective work has opened to me and there are many who oppose me (1 Corinthians 16:9).

In the light of this battle – this spiritual controversy – one of our greatest needs is to see reality and revival among God's people everywhere. If we are to fulfil the Great Commission we must see a much higher percentage of Christians really get into the action.

We don't just need more organizations, but as new ones are forming, we need to develop a more biblical and balanced view of the ministry of other groups. By being more grace-awakened we will avoid unnecessary controversy (and duplication) that drains us of strength, energy and resources needed for the work.

We don't just need more leaders. But as leadership emerges to move teams through the open doors, we need men and women with a high level of honesty, reality and integrity who will fall on their knees in obedience to the admonitions in Philippians 2:3: 'Do nothing out of selfish ambition or vain conceit, but in humility consider others better than yourselves.'

We don't just need more workers, but they must be the right workers sent forth by prayer in accordance with Matthew 9:35–8. Those workers who come from America, Canada, Great Britain and other so-called developed countries must be willing to live a simpler, sacrificial lifestyle. At present, we are transferring too much materialistic Western cultural baggage to the foreign field. It is a counter-productive use of our resources and often a huge stumbling block to people both at home and abroad. It is not just a matter of throwing mud at the walls of the mission field and seeing what sticks. There has to be screening and training; there has to be a discerning of gifts. We need the right people in the right place at the right time. We need more workers with the mind of Christ expressed in the words of Paul, 'Who . . . made himself nothing, taking the very nature of a servant . . .' (Philippians 2:6,7).

We don't just need more churches with resources. But as God is awakening a sleeping giant, the church of Jesus Christ worldwide must make those resources of prayer and communication and finance available. The people of God must have the wisdom and courage and grace to take the risks to invest in this great forward thrust to reach the world with the gospel. They must take the steps of faith to make these resources usable in the hands of all groups who are committed to run the race and who have as their burden reaching these final frontiers. In our hearts there should be the determination that there will be no letting up until the end – until the Lord returns.

May the Lord help us maintain the love and the balance and the biblical perspective in the midst of all we do in Jesus' name.

A New Harvest Force

OM is not alone in its thinking. Rather, hundreds of organizations are joining hands in the momentous task of reaching the unreached. For God is raising a movement of excited disciples from around the world ready to go anywhere and do anything.

Worldwide, the harvest team is growing – particularly in the Two-Thirds World. (You may be familiar with the term the 'Third World', but it represents two-thirds of the world's population living on two-thirds of the earth's surface. And this 'developing world' now forms more than two-thirds of the global body of Christ.) Mission is now from everywhere to everywhere:

- A church in Mongolia was born in 1990. Within five years they sent their first two missionaries to India. Several Mongolian congregations are now sending missionaries into China and around the globe on the Operation Mobilization ships.
- One of Christendom's most cross-cultural missionary teams is a Filipino couple sent under a Singapore mission agency, supported by Indonesian churches to minister to Indians in Paraguay, South America.
- Brazil has sent out more than 4,750 missionaries, and its churches are challenging each other to send out 50,000 of their young people into cross-cultural ministry.
- Nigerian churches have sent more than 3,800 missionaries. A missions vision has continued to grow in Kenya. Over 500 Kenyans are serving cross-culturally

within Kenya or abroad and India has more than 26,000 workers ministering across the complex cultural barriers in that massive country.

- Korean missionary numbers have rapidly increased. The goal of 10,000 missionaries serving in other lands by the year 2000 was almost achieved. Korea now has 10,646 – the second-highest number of missionaries serving abroad (exceeded by the USA).

Britain's contribution to world evangelization has waned over the last 200 years. In the year 2000 there was only one Protestant missionary overseas for every 6 churches. There is widespread conviction that either the job has been done or that efforts should be concentrated on Britain's needs.

Operation World states that in 2001, there were 10,654 UK missionaries in 198 different countries. But regardless of how many commit to missions in the twenty-first century, this new harvest force won't go (or worse, will go and not be as effective) unless they are sent.

In secular war, there is an acknowledged ratio of support personnel to frontline soldiers. In World War II, the military ratio was generally fifteen to one. In more recent conflicts, the ratio was expanded to 50 support workers per frontline soldier.

Spiritual warfare, which all true missionary work is, demands no less an emphasis on support personnel. In the 1700s, the Moravians of Central Europe enlisted their senders for each goer. In the Student Volunteer Movement, a massive army of 20,000 frontline missionaries were sent out. But in that same God-inspired movement, there were 80,000 committed to care for those who went. If the twenty-first century harvest force is to grow by thousands of new missionaries, the sending force must grow proportionately by tens of thousands.

Look What God is Doing in His Harvest Field Today

To understand the significance of a sending ministry, we need to see how it fits into the big picture of what God is doing. The message of the gospel never changes, but the 'all things to all men so that by all possible means . . .' (1 Corinthians 9:22) do change. For example, the following factors are affecting the methods God is using to reap a twenty-first century harvest:

- Restricted access countries are increasing, making harvest labourers more creative in their entry as students, business entrepreneurs – even tourists.
- Short-term missions is getting strategic. Increasingly, their efforts are being integrated carefully into long-term strategies on the field. For example, a missionary in a restricted country had tried without success for five years to meet the leaders of his target city. When he hosted for just one week a team of professionals from his home country, the leaders of the city openly welcomed them. As the missionary followed up on the group's contact, he exclaimed, 'This team opened more doors in one week than I had opened in five years!'
- The harvest field isn't primarily rural anymore. Over 50 per cent of the world's population now live in cities. Mass media blankets huge populations, and many times displaced people groups are more open to the gospel than when they had lived in their rural homelands.
- Technology is being used as never before. The JESUS film, a drama portraying the events of the Gospel of Luke, has been viewed by about 3 billion people. The goal of translating the script into every language spoken by 50,000 people had virtually been achieved

by 2001. This film alone has yielded over 128 million enquirers. Email and the Internet have truly connected the world into a global village!

David Bryant, executive director of Concerts of Prayer International, says in his book *The Hope at Hand* (Baker Books, 1995), 'There's an explosion of spiritual harvest around the world such as the Church has never seen before.' Let's look at some of the highlights:

- Every day across the world another 74,000 are added to the body of Christ!
- Jordan is among about thirty other countries (including Panama, Croatia and Papua New Guinea) that have mandated Bible teaching in their public schools.
- The Alpha Course phenomenon has spread across the UK to nearly every denomination and across the world as one of the most successful outreach programmes run by churches in the UK today. About 64,000 congregations were using the Alpha courses in 1998 with over 650,000 individuals having completed one.
- In 1989 there may have been only four Mongolian Christians. By 2000 there was an average of 4,000–5,000 gathering on any given Sunday, with a worshipping community of 8,000–10,000 in over 60 churches and about 100 other informal groups around the country.
- In one decade, more than 30 million in Russia came to faith in Jesus Christ.
- The church in Kazakhstan is mushrooming. For example, a Russian gave a Bible to a young Kazakh called Yerkinbek, who introduced his brother Aitkali to Christ. Aitkali led scores of young Kazakhs to Jesus. One of those was Bakitbek. He led eight others to Christ before he even knew there was an Apostle Paul.

One of the eight was his sister Kunai, who introduced dozens of university students to Jesus. So during a brief span of 18 months, six generations of new believers were born. In Almaaty more than 800 Kazakhs found new life in Christ in one year.

- In Brasilia, Brazil, 40 small congregations joined together to send their first missionary team.
- There are now more than 10,000 Spanish-speaking churches in the United States. Ethnic churches, of many languages, are in every major city.
- In Baghdad one church grew from 250 to 1,200 members in five years. Though many reports from Middle Eastern countries are often cloaked in disguised terms, victory is being told as men and women, embarrassed and frustrated by their religious and political leadership, are trusting in Christ in numbers beyond all previous records.
- The Bible is now freely available in Russia, after years of costly 'smuggling'. Between one million and two million Bibles are printed and distributed each year.
- The number of Christians in Asia has increased from 22 million (2.3 per cent) in 1900 to over 300 million (8.3 per cent) in the year 2000.
- Before World War II there was only one functioning evangelical congregation in Albania. By the end of 1992 there were over 1,000 believers gathering regularly in 19 congregations and 17 home fellowship groups. By 2000 there were over 55 denominations in over 130 congregations and 55 emerging groups.
- Believers in Uruguay initiated a National Day of Prayer – purposely set on 31 October – Halloween!
- The growth of the church in Zambia was helped in the 1990s by President Chiluba's public Christian confession and the opening up of public institution and media to the gospel. There were 515,000

evangelicals (9 per cent) in 1980. This had grown to 2.2 million (25 per cent) in 2000.

- Marches for Jesus – city-wide demonstrations declaring the Lordship of Christ – have involved millions of believers around the world. The newspaper heading in El Alto, Bolivia, read after one march: 'Jesus Summons a Bigger Crowd Than the Political Parties!'
- The AD2000 and Beyond Movement launched in 1989 proved to be the most global, focused movement for world evangelization that there ever has been. Its ministry came to an end in January 2001 according to its charter, but the effects will impact the twenty-first century. It was a co-ordinating network of many of the more activist evangelical bodies around the world. Its goals were, 'The gospel for every person and a church for every people.'
- In 2005 the Global Day of Prayer saw 200 million Christians gathering to pray for the nations.

This is good news!

However, with the princes of this world infusing only bad news into much of the Western media, most European and North American churches are discouraged about the increasing encroachment of evil. But where the darkness of sin is abounding, grace is much more abounding. What God is doing today in today's harvest field echoes Habbakuk 1:5, 'Look at the nations and watch – and be utterly amazed. For I am going to do something in your days that you would not believe, even if you were told.'

Where the Church has been planted, it has grown like wildfire. For example, just over a century ago true believers represented 2.5 per cent of world population. Then in 1970 that percentage doubled to 5 per cent of a much larger world population. Then it took 22 years to double again; in 1992 true believers represented 10 per cent of an even larger world population. Christianity is now truly a global religion. In 2000 it was estimated that 59.4 per cent of the world were Christians.

And as it grows, it is reaching across language, racial and cultural barriers to unreached people groups. God has raised up Surinam missionaries to go to the Muslims of North Africa, Chinese believers to settle among unreached Tibetans, and thousands of Indian evangelists to target the unreached ethnic groups in India. The Good News is breaking out worldwide!

And we see only the tip of the iceberg of our Heavenly Father's business these days. His perspective is infinitely deeper and broader.

To better understand and find our part as senders in this awesome task of world evangelization, we must continue to look at the bigger picture of God's purpose on earth in terms of bridging cultural distinctives and establishing strong, evangelizing churches to 'preach the gospel where Christ [is] not known' (Romans 15:20). We must ask, 'What is the remaining task?'

The Final Frontiers

Missiologists have researched and determined approximately 24,000 people groups in the world. Roughly half of the world's population live in 12,000 'reached' people groups. This does not mean all these individuals are Christians; it simply means they live in people groups where it's possible for them to respond to a clear presentation of the gospel from within their own culture in their own language.

Thus, the other half live in about 12,000 'unreached' people groups. Neither does this mean that there are no

Christians living in these areas. It does mean that there is not a viable, Bible-believing, reproducing church.

The unreached groups are mostly located geographically in what has come to be called 'The 10/40 Window' – from West Africa across Asia between the latitudes of ten degrees north and forty degrees north.

Within this 10/40 Window are:

- Most of the world's unreached people;
- Two-thirds of the world's population, although it is only one-third of the earth's land area;
- The heart of Islam, Hinduism and Buddhism;
- Eight out of ten of the poorest of the world's poor, enduring the world's lowest quality of living.

The spiritual need staring at us from the 10/40 Window is staggering. Yet, when we grasp its significance, the next question we must ask is: What are we doing about it?

A Missions Renewal Movement

Historically, the modern movements to reach the ends of the earth with God's blessing have occurred in waves. The first wave, championed by William Carey in the late 1700s, washed upon the seacoasts of the globe's continents. The second era, spearheaded by Hudson Taylor in about 1865, thrust scores of bold and daring missionaries to the inland regions of the nations.

The launch of The AD2000 and Beyond Movement has been a more recent wave with its global focus on world evangelization. Their goal of 'The gospel for every person' brought together major networks of specialist agencies in the 1990s and focused in particular on The 10/40 Window. It is hard to measure the impact of multiple means of ministry to the unconverted – personal witness, literature, Scripture translation, Christian video, cassettes, television, the Internet to name just a few. However the cumulative effects are encouraging. *Operation World* provides the following statistics relating to some of these means:

- *Scripture translation.* Through the combined ministry of the Bible societies and Bible translation agencies, 94 per cent of the world's population have access to a New Testament in their own language or soon will through existing translation projects.
- *The World by Radio Consortium* of Christian broadcasting agencies made a commitment to provide Christian radio programming for every person on earth in a language they could understand. In practical terms, it meant ensuring weekly broadcasts in 372 mega-languages. In the 1990s, 115 languages were added, leaving only 164 with no broadcasts.

- *Many other international ministries* such as SAT-7 satellite TV coverage in the Middle East, EHC, GRN, etc. could also be added to these multiple layers of global coverage.

The focus on the 10/40 Window has been successful. In the authors' own agency, deployment in the 10/40 Window went up from 34 per cent in 1984 to over 70 per cent in 2000. Thousands of congregations have been mobilized for action and prayer too. You and thousands like you are learning about serving as senders. And change is – slowly – coming about!

A Bold Move Forward

Whilst change is coming about, there is still a need for missionaries to continue ministry in people groups that already have a church movement. For example, the Hmong people of Laos and Vietnam shifted from the 'unreached' to 'reached' status. That is, from the mid-80s to the mid-90s, 330,000 of the 500,000 Hmong population became believers in Jesus Christ. So although there is obviously an amazing explosion of the gospel affecting this entire people group, the Hmong people still need outside missionaries' help to establish training programmes, to develop their own Christian growth materials, to mentor leaders.

God will accomplish His historic purpose to 'make disciples of all the nations' – the people groups of the world (see Matthew 28:19). At the end of time Christ will be exalted with the song: 'with your blood you have purchased men for God from every tribe and language and people and nation' (Revelation 5:9). No man knows that day or hour, but we live in exciting times of opportunity.

Today there are nearly 2,000 million worldwide who claim to follow Jesus Christ. *Operation World* counted 143,000 cross-cultural missionaries and 104,000 missionaries serving in their homelands – with many more working 'under the radar'. It's obvious that the body of Christ now has millions of congregations to impact their own cultures, reach the unreached and serve churches in other cultures.

If some will go. If some will serve as senders.

Full Circle

The Great Commission will be fulfilled. Jesus Christ will offer the blessing of redemption to every nation. From every people group there will be those discipled in Christ's commandments. And to accomplish His historic purpose, God will use a harvest force of goers and senders. As Mordecai said to Esther, 'Who knows but that you have come to royal position for such a time as this?' (Esther 4:14). So, we also, have the privilege to participate in this hour of opportunity.

This challenging scenario – participating in His Great Plan of the Ages – brings us full circle back to you. You are as excited about 'a church for every people' as any mission strategist who theorizes that it can be done. You are as zealous for a thriving reproducing church in your adopted people group as the most ardent frontier missionary. You are as passionate as the most effective full time evangelist about seeing the lost from every tongue and tribe finding new life in Christ. You are as diligent to see God's people discipled in Christian living as any teacher of the Word. But your zeal and passion have been tempered with the knowledge from God that, at least for now, you are to stay right where you are, actively participating in your local church.

In this chapter we have focused our attention on OM's part in the big picture of reaching the unreached. Let's superimpose this plan of 'going where the Gospel has not been preached' over the grid of the six sending responsibilities of a support team. What additional activities for involvement will this thrust provide for you?

Moral Support: Learn all you can about unreached people groups. Keep up-to-date with what is being done to develop and deploy the teams needed. Sign up to OM's various newsletters. For more information about OM, write to the office nearest you or visit www.om.org. (See the list of offices on page 188–90.)

When you hear of a person interested in going to the mission field, encourage him to focus on one of the two thrusts of cross-cultural ministry: training Two-Thirds Word nationals to reach the unreached or taking the bold Pauline drive to the ends of the earth!

Read Joshua 1. Listen to God's continual encouragement to Joshua to 'be strong and courageous' (verse 6). Again, 'Be strong and very courageous . . .' (verse 7). Yet again, 'Be strong and courageous. Do not be terrified; do not be discouraged' (verse 9). And then, as the people follow God's example, you shout the encouragement, 'Only be strong and courageous!' (verse 18).

Logistics Support: If you hold some position (formal or informal) to influence the decision-makers of your church, encourage them to establish corporate mission policies that reflect the two-pronged thrust for training Two-Thirds World nationals and frontier-focused teams. This can be done most directly through the kinds of cross-cultural workers and types of missions your church will support.

Prominently display literature and posters that encourage reaching the unreached. Any OM office can help supply you. On your church's map of the world, trace the 10/40 Window. Highlight any missionaries you have working in that area or that are training Two-Thirds World nationals to go to that area. Place a small mirror in one of the oceans. Caption it with, 'Where in the world do *you* belong?'

Look within your church for the cross-cultural 'parts' and mobilize them to become part of reaching the unreached.

Financial Support: Until you have a specific friend moving into this type of cross-cultural ministry that you can financially support, consider directing your missionary offerings to organizations such as OM that are focusing on this massive plan of reaching the unreached. You can begin putting into practice the principles of 'living more with less'. You can encourage others to join you. These ideas can work on a personal and church level.

Prayer Support: Learn more about praying for unreached people groups through *Operation World* (see resources, page 212). Use this to learn about the unreached people groups. Prayerfully adopt one of these groups. Understand their lifestyle. Become aware of their religious practices. Pray knowledgeably for them. Gather a group around you for corporate prayer for the people, for the organizations that are involved with targeting that group.

Pray for the mission leaders who are challenging the body of Christ worldwide to participate in this task of world evangelization.

Spend an evening at your local library or search the Internet to look up information on the people group your missionary is working among – not just the political country he is in. Jot down findings significant to that people's needs, spiritual bondage and possible openings to the gospel. If the group is already reached and your missionary is equipping them for growth, find out how you can pray that they will become a strong sending base for their own missionaries!

Pray for your church to act more effectively/positively on the challenge of reaching the unreached.

Communication Support: If you have no friends currently on the mission field, contact the nearest OM office for the name of several workers in a particular target area. You could be an important email support to them. Contact an OM office, requesting information on how you can send Bibles, Bible correspondence material, books or tracts to pre-selected homes of unreached peoples in various countries.

Don't forget the children. They could email the children of missionaries who are living and ministering among the peoples of the world.

Re-entry Support: Review our last chapter and remind yourself of the critical needs of missionaries returning from other cultures. Most totally unreached ethnic groups are especially different from Western culture, so re-entry stress is likely to be accentuated in these frontier mission workers. Be an active listener as they process all they experienced.

But the experience they've gained and the unique information they've acquired is particularly important for the home church – for intelligent prayer and strategic planning. Welcome these returning workers into your home and your life. Let them share what they have been learning with your home group or at your church. Have their story written up in your local newspaper. Get them to share in schools and civic organizations. Give them that opportunity for debriefing and for spreading the news of what God is doing in these final hours of history!

If your church has not yet been challenged by the forward-thrusting work of OM – bringing hope to the peoples of the world – call your nearest OM office to book a speaker or select a video. Take that first step to opening your church's world to the big picture!

(In addition to the individual study below, see the **Group Leader's Guide** for session eight beginning on page 206).

For Your Personal Involvement

- Read the story of Esther. (It's just a short book.) Pay particular attention to Mordecai's challenge to her when she was hesitant about going in to the king (Esther 4:13–14). As history records, Esther fitted into God's plan and purpose for her. She truly was called to the kingdom for such an hour as that. Throughout the Word men and women fulfilled His will for their lives and found their place in God's Hall of Faith (Hebrews 11). Mordecai's question, reverberating down through the corridors of time, heard clearly by some generations, ignored by others, is sounding a challenge to you today – a challenge to recognize that you have been called to the kingdom for an hour such as this! It is time to give serious, prayerful consideration: has God placed a call on your life to serve as a sender?
- Reaching the unreached is such a fast-paced move of God that it is making yesterday's headlines look like ancient history. Because of this, contact some of the organizations listed in Resources page 215, to get current information on global breakthroughs among unreached peoples. Be prepared to share those

highlights with your fellowship group. Check the Internet for even more up-to-date information.

Action Steps

This is it! A decision for personal involvement cannot be put off any longer! By the time you have read chapter eight, completed the 'For Your Personal Involvement' section and participated in a discussion group, you should:

- Be able to decide if serving as a sender is the part of the body of Christ that God has divinely established for you for right now. You might remember that in the very beginning we did say that if, having read and studied this book, you know that serving as a sender is *not* what God is calling you to do, that is a good decision. Move on now to find and actively involve yourself in those 'good works, which God prepared in advance for us to do', for you are 'God's workmanship, created in Christ Jesus' for that purpose (Ephesians 2:10).
- If you *do* sense God's calling on your life to serve as a sender but still have not decided on one or other of the six sending responsibilities – or if you would like to do everything, go back over the 'For Your Personal Involvement' sections to review each chapter. Find someone who knows you well who you can talk to, particularly about the giftings and abilities that seem to be the qualifications for each category.
- If you have heard His confirmation and have found one or more areas in which to serve as a sender, actively, aggressively pursue and develop this calling. Begin with the ideas given in this book, but don't be

limited by them. Be creative. Expand your capacity to serve. Allow His genius to surge through you for, after all, 'we have the mind of Christ' (1 Corinthians 2:16).

- Go back to the 'For Your Personal Involvement' section of Chapter One, on page 14. If, when you were considering that chapter, you were not able to fill in the statement of the vital importance of serving as a sender (page 17), reread those Scriptures and prayerfully complete that statement now.

- Involve others. Having a clear purpose in your own heart and mind, actively seek others in your fellowship who will bind themselves with you in the task of serving as senders. Look for vibrant Christians who don't seem to 'fit in' anywhere. It is quite possible they are looking for an opportunity like this. Share the six sending responsibilities with them.

'For "Everyone who calls on the name of the Lord will be saved. How then can they call on the one they have not believed in? And how can they believe in the one of whom they have not heard? And how can they hear without someone preaching to them? And how can they preach unless they are sent?"' (Romans 10:13–15).

Epilogue

Serving as Senders barely scratches the surface of your potential involvement in caring for your cross-cultural workers.

Selected resources follow to give you more insight into this broad subject. But beyond all that you may acquire in your reading is the practical experience you will develop as you become involved in serving as a sender.

We would certainly appreciate hearing about your successes (and failures) as you put into practice the gifts of service God has given you. To God be all glory! You can contact Operation Mobilization at one of the following addresses. You may also wish to visit www.om.org for links to other OM websites and contact addresses.

Operation Mobilization UK
The Quinta
Weston Rhyn
Oswestry
Shropshire
SY10 7LT
UK
0044(0)1691 773388
Email: contact@UK.om.org

OM Australia
PO Box 32
Box Hill
Victoria 3128
Australia
0061 9898 9348
Email: info@au.om.org

OM Canada
212 West Street
Port Colborne
Ontario
Canada
L3K 4E3
001 905 835 2546
Email: info@cdn.om.org

OM New Zealand
PO Box 72914
Papakura 1730
New Zealand
00 64 298 9990
Email: info@n2.om.org

OM Singapore
68 Lorong 16, Geylang
03–06 Association Building
Singapore 398889
00 65 6743 1889
Email: info@sgp.om.org

OM South Africa
Private Bag X04
Lynnwood Ridge
0040 Pretoria
South Africa
00 27 807 0161

OM USA
PO Box 444
Tyrone
GA 30290-0444
USA
01 770 631 0432

If you would like to know more about Emmaus Road International you can contact Mike Frith as below:

Mike Frith, OSCAR
Wotton House
Horton Road
Gloucester
GL1 3PT
UK
Tel: 0044 1452 308189
Email: info@oscar.org.uk
Web: www.oscar.org.uk

Group Leader's Guide

Chapter One: The Need for Senders

After prayer, summarize the chapter:

- From Beth's story, what obviously was wrong?
- Neither she nor her pastor were aware of the critical issue of coming back home.

  - Beth was not given (nor did she take) any opportunity to debrief – to communicate the depth of her experiences.
  - Beth may have overestimated her role in missions involvement.
  - Her friends didn't detect the symptoms of the trauma she was experiencing.

- Paul was a missionary statesman par excellence. Everything we do today to support our missionaries should find its foundation in Scripture.
- From Romans 10:13–15, it is clear that those who serve as senders share an equal responsibility and privilege with those who go. (See also John 13:16.)
- Psalm 139:14 says it succinctly: 'I am fearfully and wonderfully made.' The integrated yet extremely

complex personality of your cross-cultural worker will be stripped of every comfort zone he has come to appreciate, as he grapples with the various stages of ministry experience. Because of this, he needs an active, knowledgeable and committed support team while preparing to go, while on the field and when he returns home.

- Each area of support has its unique responsibilities and is best served by specific giftings within the body of Christ.
- What this book is encouraging every mission-minded church to do is being demonstrated by an average-sized church in Sacramento.

Go over the 'For Your Personal Involvement' section:

- Help the group see the progression of Paul's linear logic establishing the *senders* as foundational to the goal of the salvation of the lost! It is true that the further we are away from the actual action of praying the 'sinner's prayer', the more difficult it is to feel a part of it. Perhaps a couple's experience at being far from the front line could help illustrate:

We served for a time with Wycliffe Bible Translators in the jungles of Peru. My wife was assigned to keeping an inventory of the radio parts. For her, a full-time 'people-person', this took some discipline! By tracing the sequence from radio parts to the actual goal of Wycliffe, we were more able to rejoice in such a task. Somebody had to keep up the inventory of radio parts so the radio men could keep the plane radios in repair so the pilots could fly the linguists to the village so the linguists could translate the Bible so the indigenous people could have a culturally relevant presentation of the gospel of Christ so they could put their trust in him and be saved!

- Make sure the nine stages and the incidents in time that mark the transition from one to another are clearly understood.
- Read the six passages of Scripture that parallel the six support responsibilities. Make sure everyone sees the application of the Scripture.
- Discuss the value of specific giftings for the specific areas of support.
- Pray for those who have committed themselves to a study of this book. Ask the Lord for clear insight into which area of support each should become committed to. Or, if specific cross-cultural support is not their function in the body of Christ, pray that that will be equally clear.

For Further Action

- Given the structure of your church, how can you elevate the importance of the ministry of serving as senders?
- Do the missionaries supported by your fellowship or by you know of these six areas of service available to them? You might want to consult your missionaries. Get them to place the six support ministries in priority. Further, have them rate on some scale from excellent to poor how adequate they think their support is in each area. Careful! If they are honest with you, what they say may hurt!
- From this report, decide on clear, deliberate steps to take in order to reinforce the areas of care they sense are lacking.

Chapter Two: Moral Support

After prayer, summarize the chapter:
  From Scott and Jean's story:

- God is not the author of confusion, so obviously someone 'heard' wrong.
- Commitment as senders is mandatory.
- Support from more than one fellowship is vital.

From the biblical accounts:

- We see how the lack of moral support is common in humans.
- It will take the wisdom of God and conscious effort to reverse the trend.

From the foundation stones:

- Jesus is our example in word and deed as the Chief Cornerstone.
- Do it simply – and simply do it!
- Moral support is a two-way street.
- Active listening is vital to moral support.
- Commissioning – the call confirmed, the strategy determined and the 'laying on of hands' is vital.

From building awareness:

- There are plenty of resources to encourage and challenge toward moral support.

Go over the 'For Your Personal Involvement' section:

- Ask several people to share their meditations on various translations of Matthew 12:20.
- Have a 'teaser-length' (1-2 minute) book review of one or more of the books listed or others that have been read.
- Identify the kinds of people who can give solid moral support.
- Get several people to read their rewritten story.
- Discuss some of this world's philosophies – whether by bumper sticker, commercial jingles or other sources of input – that can distract us from giving moral support.

Pray for those who have made the commitment actively to encourage the body of Christ. Pray for those who are still uncertain of their place in ministry.

For Further Action

- Contrast Joseph's initial response in Matthew 1:18–19 with Elizabeth's first words to Mary on her visit (Luke 1:39–45).
- Role-play various non-supportive, then supportive responses to the following situations:

  - Somebody telling their parents that they think God wants them to go on a two-year mission trip.
  - Somebody telling their best friend that their parents are angry that they believe God wants them to go on a two-year mission venture.
  - An assistant pastor telling his pastor that a missionary society has invited him to go on a two-year mission venture.
  - Design your own role play!

Chapter Three: Logistics Support

After prayer, summarize the chapter:

- From the story you can emphasize that nobody can do everything. But as everybody does something the job will get done!
- Both the Bible and growing missionary society practices are placing the responsibility for initiating the missions process on the local church.

  - Identify the cross-cultural parts of your fellowship.
  - Give them opportunity to exercise their gifts by being involved in a missions fellowship, by working with internationals in your home town and by going on a mini-mission.
  - Check the accountability of the ministry with which they will work.
  - Confirm their spiritual maturity and growth before they go, while they are gone, and when they come home.
  - Establish good business practices governing all aspects of your missionary's affairs. If your missionary is going through a missionary society, you as the sending church still need to be aware of their policies and where you fit in.

- There are innumerable details that can be handled by a group of individuals.

  - How should their material goods be handled?
  - Are there family matters to be taken care of?
  - What ministry needs can be met?

- The body of Christ needs to care for its members by showing diligence, concern for details, punctuality and sound business practice.

Go over the 'For Your Personal Involvement' section:

- Discuss how to overcome the strong individualistic tendencies of our culture. How can we become more involved as the body of Christ in each other's lives?
- Compile a master list from all the logistical needs each person wrote. Don't be overwhelmed! No one person will have all of these needs, but a list like this emphasizes the diversity of needs and the vitality of logistics support.

Pray for those who have made a commitment to be a part of the Logistics Support Team for their missionary. Pray for those who have not yet made a commitment to any area of support.

For Further Action

- Consider the last missionary your church sent out. Who in the group knows which and to what degree the various logistical needs of that person are being met by your fellowship?
- Consider the internationals who live among us. What loss do they sense in not knowing how to establish all the logistics of 'setting up' in a new culture. What can you do to help them?

Chapter Four: Financial Support

After prayer, summarize the chapter:

- From the story you can emphasize God's faithfulness in supplying financial support to ministries He directs. When senders diligently seek God for His direction in helping to support missionaries financially He is faithful to provide the funds – possibly by very unusual methods!
- Typical methods of fundraising do generate some working capital. But for the long haul, more basic issues of financial management must be addressed:

  - *Giving*. The biblical principle of tithing yields to cheerful giving that grows in obedience so there is equality. Wise giving carefully chooses who and what to support.
  - *Lifestyle*. Living more with less is an exciting, viable option.
  - *Managing money overseas*. By more carefully supporting economical, effective missionary strategy, you free up money for other decisive cross-cultural work.
  - *Managing wealth back home*. Careful co-operation in any of the many money-saving schemes can free up funds for missions.

Go over the 'For Your Personal Involvement' section:

- From Scripture, discuss the philosophy of financial support the Apostle Paul seems to have adopted.
- Tithing is one principle of the Kingdom of God. It works!
- Encourage discussion about the five propositions on pages 73–4. Avoid condemnation either of yourselves or others; however, allow the Holy Spirit His opportunity to convict in the area of our wealth.

- Media input first sells us our needs, then provides us with the plastic money to mortgage our future. Get someone to come and do a talk on the biblical principles regarding the use of money.

Pray for those who have made a commitment to be a part of a missionary's Financial Support Team and for those who are still uncertain as to their personal involvement in serving as a sender.

For Further Action

- Do a study on the financial accountability of the organizations with which your missionaries are working.
- Do a study on the financial accountability of your missionaries.

Chapter Five: Prayer Support

After prayer, summarize the chapter:

- From Helen Mollenkof's story, it is clear that commitment to prayer is not to be lightly regarded; rather, it is a discipline of long-term obedience.
- Though the efficacy of prayer is a divine mystery, the practice of prayer is as clear as any Bible story.
- Prayer is the arena of spiritual warfare. Only the well-advised should enter there.
- The prayers of the Bible can serve as models for our prayers. These prayers provide for us the language and nature of petitions in line with the heart of God.

- Prayer with fasting is a powerful weapon in the spiritual warfare we are facing with our cross-cultural worker.
- 'In-the-gap' praying is a level of intercession that demands a depth of commitment beyond the novice.
- 'The harvest is plentiful but the workers are few' is as true today as when Jesus spoke it. Therefore, 'Ask the Lord of the harvest to send out workers' (Matthew 9:37-8).
- Pray that the gospel, in a culturally-relevant context, will be presented to all peoples.
- Pray that the 'strong man' will be bound.
- Pray for the coming of God's Kingdom to the hearts of all people.

Go over the 'For Your Personal Involvement' section:

- Discuss the types of prayers the group has been used to praying.
- Discuss several model prayers of Jesus and other Bible characters that have been studied, and what differences the group anticipates in their praying now.
- Ask someone to prepare and give a book review of *God's Chosen Fast* (see Resources, page 212).
- Make available the addresses of your church's missionaries for those who are ready to make a commitment to their prayer support.

Pray for those who have made a commitment to be a part of a cross-cultural worker's Prayer Support Team. Pray for those who have yet to make a commitment to any area of support.

For Further Action

- Begin a mission prayer group, or increase awareness of the existing one(s).
- Give a more prominent visual place to the prayer requests of your missionaries by:

  - Posting letters on the church notice board with prayer requests highlighted.
  - Putting excerpts of those requests in the church notice sheet each week or month.
  - Requesting regular public, congregational prayer for specific needs of your missionaries.

- Expand the vision of your church's outreach by using a world prayer guide such as *Operation World* (see Resources, pages 212).
- Prayer support is the most vital of the six areas.

  - History tells of many who forged their way to God's chosen fields of the world without moral support. But they got there.
  - Having one or more friends back home handling all of the logistics support eases the mind of the cross-cultural worker. But they have survived without it.
  - Financial support does provide conveniently for the worker's needs. But the belt can be tightened.
  - News from a far country provides great communication support. But loneliness can be handled.
  - Re-entry support certainly shores up the unstable as they come back home. But life goes on.

These five areas of support relate to the physical, emotional and psychological realms. Though the adjustments for lack of support in these areas are difficult, they can be made.

However, prayer support moves into the realm of the spiritual where there is no adjustment for lack of support! Therefore, make this issue the highest priority.

Chapter Six: Communication Support

After prayer, summarize the chapter:

- From the Paris missionary's story:
  - God is merciful, but there is a better part of wisdom that says missionaries should get some good, practical training.
  - Working with nationals enabled her to stay in the country.
  - It was fortunate for her to see a positive example.
- From Mary's story:
  - Even returning missionaries face difficulties that are helped by communication support.
  - The encouragement of communication support doesn't always take away the difficulty, but it certainly helps your missionary through it.
- From the biblical writers:
  - Make the communication real.
  - Be personal.
  - Even short letters should be written and sent.
  - Communication support is for their benefit.
  - Don't feel you have to say everything you know.
  - Reminders are good.
  - Sometimes your communication might be a God-inspired exhortation.
- Get everyone involved in letter writing.

- Be sure the content is worth reading.
- Use other means of communication as appropriate: phone, fax, email, telex, ham radio, photos, video, audio tapes, care parcels, CDs, VCDs, DVDs, visits.

Go over the 'For Your Personal Involvement' section:

- Get several people to share their highlighted letter of Paul. What was mundane in the letter – yet important enough to be included in Scripture? What did some of the other writers talk about?
- Make a list as the group relates the many different types of communication support missionaries have received.
- What have other churches found to be practical ways towards communication support?
- Compile a list of the resources within your group for communication support.

Pray for those who have made the commitment to be a part of a missionary's Communication Support Team. Pray for those who have not yet made a decision regarding any area of support.

For Further Action

- Give each person present a half sheet of paper to write a personal note to your missionary. Gather them into one envelope and post it – tonight!
- Prepare a chart to show what time it is where your missionary is living and the best times to reach them by telephone.
- Talk with the children's leader. Develop a plan for children to write to missionary children in other countries.

Chapter Seven: Re-entry Support

After prayer, summarize the chapter:

- From the seminary director's story:
  - The devastation of this missionary's 'crash' spreads far beyond the circle of his immediate family.
  - No doubt many factors beyond re-entry stress contributed to his 'spiritual suicide'. But if he had had a good Re-entry Support Team to unload on, what grief might have been averted!
- From the Situation of Re-entry:
  - Re-entry shock is the initial response and deals more with environmental changes your worker must face.
  - Re-entry stress deals more with the deeper struggles of attitude and spiritual motivation that run contrary in the two cultures.
- From the Challenge of Re-entry:
  - Become very familiar with these nine areas. It is in one or more of them that you will sense some struggle in your returning cross-cultural worker.
  - Know your worker well. Think beyond the examples given to specific issues that might frustrate them upon re-entry.
- From the Re-entry Behaviour patterns:
  - Alienation, condemnation and reversion sometimes provide the degenerative spiral down to the fourth, the ultimate escape. Be aware of these and if you notice the signs, try to divert the returned missionary from this destruction.
  - The focus of your re-entry programme should be on the fifth pattern: integration!
  - Integration is on two levels: the immediate needs of living and long-range interaction.

- The most vital, immediate issue on either level is the need for active listening.
- The Re-entry Support Team must provide opportunities for debriefing. This is as much for your worker's benefit as it is for the edification of the group listening.
- In time, slowly help your worker become involved in some meaningful level of ministry.
- Consider the specific needs of the various family members or single adult.

Go over the 'For Your Personal Involvement' section.

- Review any articles on the subject of re-entry.
- Listen to the real stories of re-entry given by returned missionaries.
- Develop a plan for educating church members on this area of support.

Pray for those who have made the commitment to be a part of their missionary's Re-entry Support Team. Pray for those who have not yet made a decision regarding any area of support.

For Further Action

- Purchase *The Re-entry Team* and read it.
- Obtain materials used by various international corporations when they bring their employees home. Incorporate transferable material to your programme of re-entry.
- In the opening chapter of this book, we related Beth's story in which she was so distraught by her lack of re-entry support that she chose to take her own life. By

God's mercy, that plan was thwarted. Unfortunately, there are other less final but equally serious forms of suicide that may require professional help. If it appears that a returning missionary is not responding to the care you are able to provide, there is a growing network of people who can help.

OSCAR is the UK information service for world missions, offering specialized services for returning missionaries, including re-entry help, counselling and information about various courses and retreats. To find out more contact OSCAR in one of the following ways: Website: www.oscar.org.uk; Email: info@oscar.org.uk or Phone: 00 44 1452 308189.

● There may be members of your fellowship who would like to participate in a broader hospitality ministry to missionaries. Makahiki Ministries is dedicated to providing short-term hospitality housing around the world for missionaries. To find out how you can help missionaries find a respite from their hectic pace, contact Makahiki Ministries, PO Box 415, Mariposa, CA 95338; Phone: 001 209 966 2988; Email: makahiki@sierratel.com; Website: www.hospitalityhomes.org.

Chapter Eight: Your Part in the Big Picture

After prayer, summarize the chapter:

● Leaders in the global Christian community are taking bold, dynamic steps to mobilize and deploy thousands of new missionaries to reach the unreached.

- God is doing a mighty work among the nations. Yet about half of the earth's population lives beyond a simple, culturally relevant presentation of the gospel.
- Most of the world's 12,000 unreached people groups live in a geographic region called the 10/40 Window.
- Until recently, very little has been done to target these people.
- They can be reached by a two-pronged attack:

  1) God is sovereignly raising up an army of new Two-Thirds nationals to go as missionaries to the unreached. Thousands can be sent to teach Two-Thirds World nationals the Word in such a way that they will teach others. (Read 2 Timothy 2:2.)
  2) Identify, mobilize, train and deploy thousands of 'Pauline-bold' teams to penetrate these final frontiers of unreached peoples.

- The body of Christ worldwide now has the resources to 'make disciples of every nation' – of every people group.
- As part of this worldwide move, we can actively serve as senders in the six areas of support as they relate to reaching the unreached.

Go over the 'For Your Personal Involvement' section:

- Focus on that most critical question Mordecai gave to Esther: 'Who knows but that you have come to royal position for such a time as this?' Relate and discuss other Scriptures that lay a responsibility for action on us to participate in God's Great Commission (Genesis 12:1–3; Isaiah 6:8; John 20:21; Matthew 28:18–20; Mark 16:15; James 1:22).

Pray as various people share global breakthroughs on what God is doing to reach every people.

For Further Action

Contact your nearest OM office (see pages 188–9 for addresses) and learn how you can be a partner with Operation Mobilization in reaching the unreached.

Resources

Books for Further Study

Contact your church, denomination or nearest OM office for their mission vision resources. It is best to keep your vision in line with the goals of your church.

Following is a list of current (and classic books) highly recommended by the missions community. It would be good for them to be in your church's library. These books may be available from 1) your local Christian bookstore, 2) www.wesleyowen.com or 3) the publisher listed.

Motivation for Missions

A Mind for Missions, Paul Borthwick (NavPress). Learn how to make God's passionate heart for the world a part of your daily life.

From Jerusalem to Irian Jaya: A Biographical History of Christian Missions, Ruth Tucker (Zondervan). An excellent 'thumbnail' history of missions.

Let the Nations be Glad!, John Piper (Baker Books). Worship, the ultimate goal of the church, fuels missions. Missions is, because worship is not.

The George Verwer Collection, George Verwer (Authentic Media). Three classic books for the price of one in this collection by George Verwer, whose writings have inspired and encouraged thousands in their Christian discipleship.

The Great Omission – A Biblical Basis for World Evangelism, Robertson McQuilkin (Authentic Media). This biblically-based investigation answers the question, 'Why isn't mission a priority today?'

Strategies for Mission

101 Ways to Change Your World – Personal Evangelism That Really Makes a Difference, Geoff Tunnicliffe (Authentic Media). Practical ways to do missions today – right where you are.

A Guide to Short-Term Missions – A Comprehensive Manual for Planning an Effective Missions Trip, Leon Greene (Authentic Media). A thorough look at the challenges and blessing facing anyone preparing for a short-terms missions trip.

Eternity in Their Hearts, Don Richardson (Regal). The concept of an eternal God can be found in hundreds of cultures around the world.

Foreign to Familiar – A Guide to Understanding Hot and Cold-Climate Cultures, Sarah Lanier (McDougall). An easy to read handbook to help bridge cultural gaps.

Islam and Christian Witness, Martin Goldsmith (Authentic Media). This book offers a clear perspective of the two cultures. Goldsmith explores the changing role of the Muslim faith, examines its central beliefs, discusses areas of agreement and disagreement between Christianity and Islam, and explains how Christians can present the Gospel to Muslims.

Literature Evangelism, George Verwer (Authentic Media). If you want to know what literature can do in the lives of people and how to do it, try this book.

Marching to a Different Drummer, Jim Raymo (Christian Literature Crusade). Rediscovering missions in an age of affluence and self-interest.

Out of the Saltshaker and into the World, Rebecca Pippert (InterVarsity Press). Let your life be poured out in a way to make the world thirsty for God.

Postmission – World Mission by a Postmodern Generation, ed. Richard Tiplady (Paternoster). Addressing significant cultural changes in the West and new ways of doing missions.

Run with the Vision, Bill and Amy Stearns, Bob Sjogren (Bethany). A user-friendly look at God's plan and how to find your place in His global agenda.

Student Mission Power, (William Carey Library). Reports of the First International Congress of the Student Volunteer Movement.

Tentmakers Speak Out, Don Hamilton (TMQ Research). This book considers the advantages and difficulties of modern 'tent-making'.

The Discovery of Genesis, C.H Kang and Ethel R. Nelson (Concordia). Hidden in the ancient Chinese characters is the story of the Bible.

The Jesus Style, Gayle D. Erwin (Ronald N. Haynes Publishers). A challenge to incarnate the lifestyle of Jesus in your daily living.

The Liberating Gospel in China, Ralph Covell (Baker Books). Stories of God's love and grace during persecution.

The World at Your Doorstep, Lawson Lau (Intervarsity Press). A challenge to minister among internationals who are living among us.

Today's All Star Missions Churches – Strategies to Help Your Church Get in the Game, Tom Telford (Baker Books). A study of churches that are deeply involved in missions. Great ideas for your church.

Prayer Support

Destined for the Throne, Paul Billheimer (Bethany House). Here is a message of God's love for His Son's Bride. It is a powerful call to prayer.

God's Chosen Fast, Arthur Wallis (Christian Literature Crusade). The classic on why, when, where and how to fast.

Operation China, Paul Hattaway (Piquant). Excellent prayer information for the 490 minority groups of China. Beautiful pictures; accurate information.

Operation World – 21st Century Edition, Patrick Johnstone and Jason Mandryk (Authentic Media). This book is packed with inspiring information for prayer about every country of the world.

Piercing the Darkness, Frank Peretti (Crossway Books). The influence of the unseen world in the affairs of life are dramatically suggested in this novel, challenging us to pray.

This Present Darkness, Frank Peretti (Crossway Books). A wild fantasy of the unseen battle between good and evil, challenging us to prayer.

Touch the World Through Prayer, Wesley Duewel (Zondervan). Each chapter will teach you about the power of intercessory prayer.

Windows on the World – When We Pray God Works, Daphne Spraggett and Jill Johnstone (Authentic Media). Stunning photographic visuals illustrate information and prayer points for 100 countries and people groups.

Re-entry Support

Culture Shock, Myron Loss (Light and Life Press). Learn how your missionary needs to deal with the stress of cross-cultural living.

The Re-entry Team – Caring for Your Returning Missionaries, Neal Pirolo (Emmaus Road Intl.). Through 70 case studies, the Church learns how to serve in this most neglected area of missionary care.

To Understand Each Other, Paul Tournier (Westminster John Knox). How to reverse the trend that most conversations of the world are 'dialogues of the deaf'.

We Really Do Need to Listen, Reuben Welch (Impact Books). In his unique style, the author brings to light the greatest need in human relationship.

Financial Support

Friend Raising – Building a Missionary Support Team That Lasts, Betty Barnett (YWAM Publishing). Vital help for those building their support team. An excellent counterpart of this book, *Serving As Senders.*

Living More With Less, Doris Janzen Longacre (Herald Press). Learn how to enhance your lifestyle while spending less money.

Inspiring Stories of Missions and Missionaries

A Distant Grief, F. Kefa Sempangi (Regal). An African pastor's poignant account of a nation destroyed by a godless murderer and his false religion.

Anointed for Burial, Todd and DeAnn Burke (Logos International). The power of God at work in the lives of Cambodian missionaries.

Bruchko, Bruce Olson (Creation House). The astonishing true story of a nineteen-year-old missionary among the Motilone Indians in South America.

By Their Blood, James and Marti Helfrey (Baker Books). A record of Christian martyrs of the twentieth century.

Chasing the Dragon, Jackie Pullinger (Hodder & Stoughton). The amazing story of breaking the bondage of opium addiction in Hong Kong.

Death of a Guru, Rabi R. Maharaj (Harvest House). Autobiography of a Hindu, destined to become a guru, who trusted in Christ instead.

I Dared to Call Him Father, Bilquis Sheikh (Chosen Books). The riveting story of a Muslim woman to whom Jesus appeared in a dream.

Lifting the Veil – A World of Muslim Women, Phil and Julie Parshall (Authentic Media). A heart-wrenching and perplexing look at the true world of Muslim women.

Lords of the Earth, Don Richardson (Regal). The incredible tale of Irian Jaya's Snow Mountains Yali people and their encounter with Christ.

Peace Child, Don Richardson (Regal). Come to understand the concept of 'redemptive analogy' through the story of the Sawi people.

Shadow of the Almighty: The Life and Testament of Jim Elliot, Elisabeth Elliot (Authentic Media). A life-challenging biography of Jim Elliot.

Tortured for His Faith, Haralan Popov (Zondervan). An epic of Christian courage under severe persecution.

Unveiled at Last, Bob Sjogren (Crown Ministries, Intl.). Exciting stories of God's unchanging purpose to redeem some from every tribe, tongue and people.

Vanya, Myrna Grant (Creation House). A true story of ruthless persecution in the Red Army and Vanya's courage through it.

Youth and Mission, Paul Borthwick (Authentic Media). A practical handbook that provides principles, guidelines and examples of how to involve youth in missions.

For Updated Search

We live in a fast-paced culture in which the landscape of our world is rapidly changing. Here are a few websites for you to browse and keep up-to-date with how we can pray for mission. Bookmark them and refer to them so that they can help you and your church to become aggressively active – intentionally engaged in the battle for lost souls.

AD2000 and Beyond Movement: www.ad2000.org
AIMS: www.aims.org
Barnabas Fund: www.barnabasfund.org
Caleb Project: www.calebproject.org
Centre for Mission Direction: www.cmd.org.nz
Dawn Ministries: www.dawnministries.org
Global Evangelization Movement: www.gem-werc.org
Global Prayer Digest: www.global-prayer-digest.org
Joshua Project: www.joshuaproject.net
The Network for Strategic Mission:
www.strategicnetwork.org
Operation Mobilization: www.om.org
OSCAR: www.oscar.org.uk
People Teams: www.peopleteams.org
World Evangelical Alliance: www.worldevangelical.org

Resources Available Through Emmaus Road International

ACTS Video/Audio Training Tapes

Prepare for Battle: Lessons in Spiritual Warfare – This nine-hour video or audio training tapes programme comes with nineteen pages of Student Notes and Assignments and a Study Guide for Groups or Individuals.

Building Your Support Team – This two-hour audio training tape is the counterpart of the book, *Serving As Senders,* instructing the missionary in how to develop relationships in the six areas of support.

Solutions to Culture Stress – This four-hour video helps prepare a short-term missionary for the culture stress of going overseas and returning home.

ACTS Tape Library – A Library of various titles.

Publications

Critical Issues in Cross-Cultural Ministry are 4-6-page bulletins written on vital missions topics. Reprints available:

Series I: *Mobilizing Your Church* 15 Issues
Series II: *For Those Who Go* 15 Issues
Series III: *Serving As Senders* 12 Issues
Series IV: *Internationals Who Live Among Us* 12 Issues

SERVING AS SENDERS: How to Care for Your Missionaries – While They are Preparing to Go, While They are on the Field, and When They Return Home.

PREPARE FOR BATTLE: Basic Training in Spiritual Warfare – Making reference to over 700 Scriptures that point to victory in battle, this book drives home the importance of practising the basics in spiritual warfare.

THE RE-ENTRY TEAM: Caring for Your Returning Missionaries – This study book focuses in on the least understood and most difficult time in the life of a missionary.

I THINK GOD WANTS ME TO BE A MISSIONARY: Issues to Deal with Long Before You Say Goodbye – This is a story lived out by four young people, their pastors and others as they grapple with real life issues facing those who believe God wants them to be a missionary.

Seminars

Nothing GOOD Just Happens! Seminar – This is an intense, 21-hour seminar to train church missions leadership in how to mobilize their fellowship in cross-cultural outreach ministry.

For Those Who Go Seminar – The sessions of this 6-hour seminar help the potential cross-cultural worker look beyond the 'romance' of missions and to deal with some very practical issues of going.

Serving As Senders Seminar – The lessons of the book are presented in a 6-hour seminar format.

What's the Big Deal? They're Just Coming Home! – This 3-hour seminar establishes from Scripture the five simply-stated steps a returning missionary must go through, the many issues that makes this a difficult process and, using real re-entry situations, examines how to overcome the difficulties.

ACTS Training Courses

ACTS Team Orientation – 2–8 hours of cultural, interpersonal relationship and spiritual warfare training for short-term teams.

ACTS Boot Camp – One week of cultural, interpersonal relationship and spiritual warfare training for those serving up to six months.

ACTS 29 Training Course – An intensive 10-week immersion in a second culture to learn how to live and minister in other cultures. The classes include cultural

adaptation, language acquisition, interpersonal relationships, spiritual warfare and how to remove from the gospel and the teachings of Christ, Western warfare, and
uncultrating the and Gospel Teachings of Christ. This
field training incorporates classroom study and community experience with living in the home of a national.

Mini-ACTS 29 Training Course – A 4-week modified
schedule of the 10-week course.

ACTS Ministry Trips

ERI leads 3-week trips throughout the year. Pre-field
training, a hands-on ministry trip, and follow-up with
individuals, helps church leaders develop a consistent
involvement in missions.

Speakers Bureau

Neal and Yvonne Pirolo, Mike Frith and other associates
of Emmaus Road, are available as speakers on a variety
of subjects, all challenging to a personal involvement in
cross-cultural outreach ministry.

For more information on these or other developing
resources to equip you and your church for cross-cultural
ministry, contact:

Emmaus Road International
7150 Tanner Court
San Diego, CA 92111 USA
001 858 292 7020
emmaus_road@eri.org
www.eri.org